# WOODSMEN
# OF THE WEST

# WOODSMEN
## OF THE WEST

by Martin Allerdale Grainger

With an Afterword by Murray Morgan

Edited by Steven T. Murray

*Illustrated*

Western Writers Series No. 2

Fjord Press
Seattle
1988

Published and distributed by
Fjord Press
P.O. Box 16501
Seattle, Washington 98116
(206) 625-9363

Original version published 1908
by Edward Arnold, London &
The Musson Book Co. Ltd., Toronto

Fjord Press recognizes that some of the racial attitudes of the
author may offend the sensibilities of today's readers, but we
have retained the original language in such cases in order to
preserve the author's authentic voice of the times.

Cover design: Art Chantry Design, Seattle
Design & typography: Fjord Press Typography, Seattle

Library of Congress Cataloging-in-Publication Data:

Grainger, Martin Allerdale, 1874–1941.
Woodsmen of the West.

(Western writers ; no. 2)
1. British Columbia — History — Fiction.
I. Murray, Steven T. II. Title. III. Series:
Western writers series (Seattle, Wash.)
PR9199.3.G688W66 1988     813'.52     88-24352
ISBN 0-940242-35-4 (alk. paper)
ISBN 0-940242-34-6 (pbk. : alk. paper)

Printed in the United States of America by Edwards Bros.
First edition, 1988

*To my creditors,*
*affectionately*

# CONTENTS

# LIST OF ILLUSTRATIONS

# WOODSMEN
# OF THE WEST

# CHAPTER I

# In Vancouver

A S YOU WALK DOWN Cordova Street in the city of Vancouver you notice a gradual change in the appearance of the shop windows. The shoe stores, drug stores, clothing stores, phonograph stores cease to bother you with their blinding light. You see fewer goods fit for a bank clerk or man in business; you leave "high tone" behind you.

You come to shops that show faller's axes, swamper's axes — single-bitted, double-bitted; screw jacks and pump jacks, wedges, sledge-hammers, and great seven-foot saws with enormous shark teeth, and huge augers for boring boomsticks, looking like properties from a pantomime workshop.

Leckie calls attention to his logging boot, whose bristling spikes are guaranteed to stay in. Clarke exhibits his Wet Proof Peccary Hogskin gloves, that will save your hands when you work with wire ropes. Dungaree trousers are shown to be copper-riveted at the places where a man strains them in working. Then there are oilskins and blankets and rough suits of frieze for winter wear, and woollen mitts.

Outside the shop windows, on the pavement in the street, there is a change in the people too. You see few women. Men look into the windows; men drift up and down the street; men lounge in groups upon the curb. Your eye is struck at once by the unusual proportion of big men in the crowd, men that look powerful even in their town clothes.

Many of these fellows are faultlessly dressed: very new boots, new black clothes of quality, superfine black shirt, black felt hat. A few wear collars.

Others are in rumpled clothes that have been slept in; others, again, in old suits and sweaters; here and there one in dungarees and working boots. You are among loggers.

They are passing time, passing the hours of the days of their trip to town. They chew tobacco, and chew and chew and expectorate, and look across the street and watch any moving thing. At intervals they will exchange remarks impassively; or stand grouped, hands in pockets, two or three men together in gentle, long-drawn-out conversations. They seem to feel the day is passing slowly; they have the air of ocean passengers who watch the lagging clock from meal-time to meal-time with weary effort. For comfort it seems they have divided the long day into reasonable short periods; at the end of each 'tis "time to comeanavadrink." You overhear the invitations as you pass.

Now, as you walk down the street, you see how shops are giving place to saloons and restaurants, and the price of beer decorates each building's front. And you pass the blackboards of employment offices and read chalked thereon:

50 axemen wanted at Alberni
5 rigging slingers $4
buckers $3½, swampers $3.

And you look into the public rooms of hotels that are flush with the street as they were shop windows; and men sit there watching the passing crowd, chairs tipped back, feet on window-frame, spittoons handy.

You hear a shout or two and noisy laughter, and walk awhile outside the curb, giving wide berth to a group of men scuffling with one another in alcohol-inspired play. They show activity.

Then your eye catches the name-board of a saloon, and you remember a paragraph in the morning's paper —

"In a row last night at the Terminus Saloon several men . . ."

and it occurs to you that the chucker-out of a loggers' saloon must be a man "highly qualified."

The *Cassiar* sails from the wharf across the railway yard Mondays and Thursdays 8 P.M. It's only a short step from the Gold House and the Terminus and the other hotels, and a big bunch of the boys generally comes down to see the boat off.

You attend a sort of social function. You make a pleasing break in the monotony of drifting up the street to the Terminus and down the street to the Eureka, and having a drink with the crowd in the Columbia bar, and standing drinks to the girls at number so-and-so Dupont Street—the monotony that makes up your holiday in Vancouver. Besides, if you are a *woodsman* you will see fellow aristocrats who are going north to jobs: you maintain your elaborate knowledge of what is going on in the woods and where everyone is; and, further, you know that in many a hotel and logging camp up the coast new arrivals from town will shortly be mentioning, casual-like: "Jimmy Jones was down to the wharf night before last. Been blowing-her-in in great shape has Jimmy, round them saloons. Guess he'll be broke and hunting a job in about another week, the pace he's goin' now."

You have informed the *Morning Post*!

If logging is but the chief among your twenty trades and professions—if you are just the ordinary western *logger*—still the north-going *Cassiar* has great interest for you. Even your friend Tennessee, who would hesitate whether to say telegraph operator or carpenter if you asked him his business suddenly—even he may want to keep watch over the way things are going in the logging world.

So you all hang around on the wharf and see who goes on board, and where they're going to, and what wages they hired on at. And perhaps you'll help a perfect stranger to get himself and two bottles of whisky (by way of baggage) up the gang-plank; and help throw Mike M'Curdy into the cargo-room, and his blankets after him.

Then the *Cassiar* pulls out amid cheers and shouted messages, and you return up town to make a round of the bars, and you laugh once in a while to find some paralysed passenger whom friends had forgotten to put aboard . . . And so to bed.

The first thing a fellow needs when he hits Vancouver is a clean-up: hair cut, shave, and perhaps a bath. Then he'll want a new hat for sure. The suit of town clothes that, stuffed into the bottom of a canvas bag, has travelled around with him for weeks or months — sometimes wetted in rowboats, sometimes crumpled in a seat or pillow — the suit may be too shabby. So a fellow will feel the wad of bills in his pocket and decide whether it's worth getting a new suit or not.

The next thing is to fix on a stopping-place. Some men take a fifty-cent room in a rooming house and feed in the restaurants. The great objection to that is the uncertainty of getting home at night. In boom times I have known men of a romantic disposition who took lodgings in those houses where there is a certain society. But that means frenzied finance, and this time you and I are not going to play the fool and blow in our little stake same as we did last visit to Vancouver.

So a fellow can't do better than go to a good, respectable hotel where he knows the proprietor and the bartenders, and where there are some decent men stopping. Then he knows he will be looked after when he is drunk; and getting drunk, he will not be distressed by spasms of anxiety lest someone should go through his pockets and leave him broke. There are some shady characters in a town like Vancouver, and persons of the under-world.

Of course, the first two days in town a man will get good-and-drunk. That is all right, as any doctor will tell you; that is good for a fellow after hard days and weeks of work in the woods.

But you and I are no drinking men, and we stop there and sober up. We sit round the stove in the hotel and read the newspapers, and discuss Roosevelt, and the Trusts, and Socialism, and Japanese immigration; and we tell yarns and talk logs. We sit at the window and watch the street. The hotel bar is in the next room, and we rise once in a while and take a party in to "haveadrink." The bartender is a good fellow, one of the boys: he puts up the drinks himself, and we feel the hospitality of it. We make a genial group. Conversation will be about loggers and logs, of course, but in light anecdotal vein, with loud bursts of laughter.

Now one or two of the friends you meet are on the bust; ceaselessly setting-up the drinks, insisting that everybody drink with them. I am not "drinking" myself: I take a cigar and fade away. But you stay; politeness and good fellowship demand that you should join each wave that goes up to the bar, and when good men are spending money you would be mean not to spend yours too.

Pretty soon you feel the sweet reasonableness of it all. A hardworking man should indemnify himself for past hardships. He owes it to himself to have a hobby of some kind. You indulge a hobby for whisky.

About this time it is as well to hand over your roll of bills to Jimmy Ross, the proprietor. Then you don't have to bother with money any more: you just wave your hand each time to the bartender. *He* will keep track of what you spend.

Now you are fairly on the bust: friends all round you, good boys all. Some are hard up, and you tell Jimmy to give them five or ten dollars; and "Gimme ten or twenty," you'll say, "I want to take a look round the saloons"—which you do with a retinue.

The great point now is never to let yourself get sober. You'll feel awful sick if you do. By keeping good-and-drunk you keep joyous. "Look bad but feel good" is sound sentiment. Even suppose you were so drunk last night that Bob Doherty knocked the stuffing out of you in the Eureka bar, and you have a rankling feeling that your reputation as a fighting man has suffered somewhat—still, never mind, line up, boys; whisky for mine: let her whoop, and to hell with care! Yah-hurrup and smash the glass!!

If you are "acquainted" with Jimmy Ross—that is to say, if you have blown in one or two cheques before at his place, and if he knows you as a competent woodsman—Jimmy will just reach down in his pocket and lend you fives and tens after your own money is all gone. In this way you can keep on the bust a little longer, and ease off gradually—keeping pace with Jimmy's growing disinclination to lend. But sooner or later you've got to face the fact that the time has come to hunt another job.

There will be some boss loggers in town; you may have been drinking with them. Some of them perhaps will be sobering up and beginning to remember the business that brought them to Vancouver, and to think of their neglected camps up-coast.

Boss loggers generally want men; here are chances for you. Again, Jimmy Ross may be acting as a sort of agent for some of the northern logging camps: if you're any good Jimmy may send you up to a camp. Employment offices, of course, are below contempt — they are for men strange to the country, incompetents, labourers, farm hands, and the like.

You make inquiries round the saloons. In the Eureka someone introduces you to Wallace Campbell. He wants a riggin' slinger: you are a riggin' slinger. Wallace eyes the bleary wreck you look. Long practice tells him what sort of a man you probably are when you're in health. He stands the drinks, hires you at four and a half, and that night you find yourself, singing drunk, in the *Cassiar*'s saloon — on your way north to work.

## CHAPTER II

# Going North

I WAS NOT SINGING DRUNK myself, nor was I on my way to securely promised work, as I stood upon the deck of the steamer *Cassiar* one evening and watched the lights of Vancouver disappear. In fact, I was depressingly sober, as it is my habit to be; and I began to think with some anxiety of my immediate affairs and to make a series of hurried calculations.

My steamer fare had cost five dollars and a half. But there was a pound of cheese and two packets of grape-nuts in my bag, and so I knew I could avoid the fifty-cent meals aboard the boat. Thus Friday night would see me landed at Hanson Island Hotel with sixteen dollars and a half in pocket.

Now on what system did they run that hotel? What would they charge? Meals would be fifty cents; that I knew. But would they throw in sleeping accommodation — bed or floor — free gratis as at Port Browning? If so, I could allow myself to eat two meals a day, and so last out for eleven days, and still have five and a half dollars for the return trip to Vancouver should that be necessary.

"Why all these considerations?" you will ask. "Why think of the return journey?"

Well, you see, my prospects were uncertain. Two months had gone since Carter had asked me to work for him. Carter might have changed his mind. Carter might be ill. Carter might have decided to shut down camp this winter. And so at Hanson Island I might find myself among strangers, with no one to give me work. Indeed, all sorts of unpleasant things might happen. I had left my last job and been laid up for several weeks on account of a damaged foot; and the foot was still troublesome. And so I could not venture to undertake any work that should require real activity. There were thus few jobs possible for me in that logging country.

Then, again, suppose Carter's steamboat should not come down from the camp to Hanson Island for one week, two weeks, three weeks. I couldn't sit on the hotel veranda for three solid weeks. Besides, I would not have the money to do it. And I felt I would be too shy to explain the situation to the hotel proprietor. It was not as if I had the certainty of work when Carter's steamer should arrive. Had I that, it would be easy to tell the hotel man to charge up my expenses to my boss. But as an utter stranger, with no certain job in view, how could I ask for credit? Jawbone is the western word for credit. I lack the art of using mine persuasively.

So it looked much as if I should have to turn tail and leave the logging country unless Carter or his boat should turn up at Hanson Island within ten days, or unless, of course, I could strike another job that would suit a man with a damaged foot. After all, Hanson Island might be in some ways an eligible centre for business purposes. . . . So I meditated; and then fell into conversation with an old fellow who, like me, preferred the open deck to the noise and stuffiness of the crowded saloon. We listened to the slap of the ripples against the steamer's bow as she thumped her way up the Gulf, and we looked into the darkness. The old fellow told me a great yarn of the early days on San Juan Island; and of how the shooting of Fluit's pigs by Cutler nearly led to war between British Columbia and the State of Washington somewhere in the 'sixties or early 'seventies; and of how, when garrisons were placed by either party on the island, he and his brother had found an opening for an ingenious system of smuggling and had made money. . . .

The wind began to feel cold and we went inside the saloon. The boat was really very quiet now. In the smoking-room there sat a coterie engaged at whisky, but at the stern their bursts of laughter and loud talk were made remote by the steady throbbing from the engine room and by the snores of sleeping men. There was no temptation to waste money on a berth, for all the little cabins were taken and several men were sleeping on the passage floors. By good luck I found a bench unoccupied, and lying down, drew some oil-skins over me and set myself to sleep. Some time in the night I remember a gentleman lifting off my covering and looking at my face. He was speechlessly drunk, I think, and he patted my head. I think I fell asleep while he was doing it... Next morning I awoke to eat my cheese and grape-nuts and to look upon a glorious dawn. The sea, in the narrow channels that we threaded, was glassy calm; except where our churning wake lay white behind us, and where the steamer's bows sent a small swell to swash against the nearby rocks. There is deep water close to shore almost everywhere along the coast.

If you take a large-scale map of British Columbia you will notice how the three-hundred-mile stretch of Vancouver Island, like a great breakwater, shuts off from ocean a fine strip of sea, and how that sea is all littered with islands. You will see the outline of the mainland coast, from Vancouver north, a jagged outline all dented with inlets and sounds and arms — fiords they call them elsewhere. Try to realise that the shores of these fiords are mostly mountain slopes, that slopes and narrow valleys and hilly islands — all the land everywhere — are covered with big forest to the very edge of tide-water, and you will have some idea of the scenery I looked upon that morning from the after-deck of the *Cassiar*.

There was green forest — and it looked like a moss upon the higher slopes; and the bristling dead poles of burnt forest showing against the bare mottled rock: standing timber, fallen timber, float-ing logs and tree tops; and drift logs piled white upon the beach. There were long stretches of coast along which, every few yards, little lanes seemed to have been cut in the water-side forest. And now we were well into the northern logging country; for these little lanes marked the work of hand-loggers, and were the paths down which big logs had crashed their way into the sea.

I let the scenery be and wandered round the ship, watching, under cover of a bored demeanour, my fellow passengers. All of us had become quiet and respectable. The barroom did no business.

Some men slept on benches, slept solid; sleeping off the after-effects of Vancouver and "life." Most of us mooned about the deck, in silence; or listened, in groups, to the conversation of those who spoke.

Some of us were obviously not loggers. One man, I think, was a lawyer going up to a camp on some business. There were one or two timber buyers — one I recognised as a man who acts as agent for a lumber company on Broughton Island.

Last summer the timber speculators and pulp-concession men persuaded the authorities to send a police launch cruising round the islands and inlets of the coast: the story was that the hand-loggers were getting logs from timber lands that had been staked — that is to say, that had become private property. The police on the launch collared a number of men and took them down for trial to Vancouver on the charge of stealing. Some of these men were now on board, returning north on bail. One man told us that day how he had been at work with his mate sawing a tree when the policeman came and

*A log shot down the mountainside by hand-loggers.*

demanded his licence; and how the policeman wouldn't let him go to his cabin (a few miles away) to fetch it, but had dragged him off then and there. The man talked of suing for damages. There was a boss logger on board who had been obliged to stop work by the police — they said he had been taking logs from a pulp-concession. The quaint thing about this is that a pulp-concession is only granted on lands where there is no timber fit for logging purposes. Someone, one supposes, has had to swear that these lands can yield no logs — and then, a year or so after, hand-loggers are prosecuted for stealing the logs whose existence has been denied!

I know nothing of the other side of the case; but on board that morning men talked freely of "graft" and "political pull." It was held to be shameful that great tracts of country should be closed against the *bona fide* logger and lie idle for the future profit of speculators.

Every now and again we would see the distant roof of a logging camp shining yellow through the trees, and hear the whistle of a donkey-engine from where white puffs of steam would show against the forest green. Then the *Cassiar* would toot and slow down, and the camp rowboat would put out to intercept us. A whole fleet of hand-loggers' boats would come out too, and tie up to the steamer's side for a few hurried minutes while meat and supplies and mail were being thrown into them. We passengers would all lean over the deck-rail above and laugh at little breakages that would occur to freight, and recognise acquaintances in the boats alongside and shout the latest news from Vancouver to them.

Down on the *Cassiar's* lower deck were rows and rows of huge quarters of beef for the camps, and piles of heavy boom chains and coils of wire cable and groceries galore, in boxes and in sacks. There were new rowboats fresh from the builders in Vancouver, and old rowboats belonging to passengers who were going timber-cruising farther north. The lower deck, in fact, was just a cargo-room, with a space partitioned off to hold the liquor and the bartender. Aft of the cargo-room were the oily-smelling engines, and the little rooms where Chinamen and Japanese cooked and washed dishes and peeled potatoes. There too was the skookum box — that is, the *strong room* or lock-up. To it the first mate of the *Cassiar* is wont to shoot too noisy drunks, pushing them before him, at arm's length, with that fine collar-and-trouserseat grip of his that is so much admired.

Just beyond Church House we lay at anchor for an hour or two, waiting for slack water in the Euclataws. The northern and the southern tides meet here, and in the narrow channel whirlpools form. There's something in the sinister, all-powerful thrust and sweep of such water that puts the fear of God into a man in a rowboat—if he is a little bit late for slack water. But of course the *Cassiar* doesn't mind going through, as long as the tide hasn't turned very long. . . .

The White Frenchman came out in his boat for supplies. In the last month, I notice, he has collected quite a few logs—all lonely himself in that dismal place. For his shack is on the mountain slope just below the rapids: the situation chosen for beach-combing purposes. When a tug towing a raft gets into trouble at the Euclataws and loses logs Auguste is sure to pick up some.

Perhaps it was the monotony of the cheese and grape-nuts (eaten within smell of tempting odours from the dining-saloon) that made the day seem dull to me; perhaps it was the vague gnawing unhappiness that a nervous person always feels when facing the uncertainty of getting work; or perhaps it was the poorness of my luck in attempting acquaintance with other men on board. I cut a feeble figure in such casual talk; the men I spoke to seemed to be duller still.

The westerner—especially the American westerner—has usually a composed and competent air. It is surprising sometimes when you have nerved yourself (after some shyness) to commence a conversation with a grim-looking stranger, to find that he is really feeling rather lonely and "out of it" in strange surroundings. There is so often a wonderful contrast between the ease of the man's appearance and the uneasiness that shows in his talk.

I noticed that I broke the ice with about ten men on board, but not a soul took the first step and addressed me. And yet some of the men I tackled proved to be desperately anxious to talk once they had been spoken to. One reason I imagined was that the great demand for men had brought an unusual number of strangers about. Another reason was that my "twang" and "broadness of speech" and queer way of expressing myself—the result of an education in England—made me strange and difficult for them to size up.

# CHAPTER III

# At Hanson Island Hotel

A T ELEVEN O'CLOCK, in the pitch darkness of that Friday night, the *Cassiar* drew near to Hanson Island and made the hilly shores of the narrow channel re-echo with her siren. We passed a dark headland and saw the lights of the hotel.

Several lanterns were flickering about along the beach, and we could judge that men were launching rowboats and hurrying to meet us at the raft. For at Hanson Island there is no wharf. A large raft anchored in the sea serves for the landing-stage; a shed built thereon serves as warehouse for the freight.

The *Cassiar's* searchlight glared upon the raft where men stood waiting to catch the mooring ropes. The steamer edged her way gingerly alongside and was made fast; the doors of the cargo-room were opened, freight was poured out upon the raft, hurriedly; and we passengers let ourselves down upon the boxes and bales that lay piled in rank confusion. All was black shadow, and dim forms and feeble lantern gleams.

I was surprised, for a moment, to find that a man had seized my blanket roll and pitched it into the far darkness; but then I found a boat was waiting there. Someone flashed a lantern; I jumped into the boat. I saw a solemn, fat old Dutchman tumble in behind me; other men came pushing in. Soon in that boat we were a solid mass of men and bundles. Then we began to move, and I heard a weak, drunken voice appealing for more room to work his oars. Heavens! I recognised those wheedling tones at once. The oarsman was my old acquaintance Jim; Jim the "engineer"; Jim, ex-coal-trimmer from the White Star Line.

My old acquaintance Jim was dreadful drunk, but not too drunk to know his duty. He held to a design to row the boat ashore, aiming for where the hotel lights shone bright above the beach. We moved through utter darkness, Jim's oars waggling feebly in the water.

Then we went bump and bump again, and reaching out our hands, we felt a floating log that barred our path. We seemed to get entangled with logs; logs everywhere. Jim, with sudden fury, tried to row over them. Then he gave up the attempt and told us to walk ashore upon the logs. But a tearful-drunk old voice wailed against the idea in foreign-sounding cockney accents, and other voices made an angry chorus, saying that their boots were not spiked and that they would walk no slippery logs in darkness, and they swore. So the engineer became absorbed again in trying to row over logs, bump, bump, bump . . . until he felt it futile and reached the querulous verge of tears . . . I jumped, thigh-deep, into the water then and took my stuff ashore, leaving the fools in drunken argument.

I opened the front door of the hotel and walked, half blinded by the dazzle of acetylene, into the public room. Noise was my first impression — noise of shuffling feet, stamp of dancing men, loud talk and shouted cuss-words. Then I saw that the room was crowded.

A red-hot stove stood in one corner, and round it men sat in chairs or stood warming themselves or drying their wet clothes. A card game was going on at a small table, and men stood around, three deep, to watch the play. Large sums were in the pool. There was an incessant coming and going of men between the barroom and the public room, and men loafed about the rooms and passages and talked, or argued, or scuffled playfully. Some danced to the tunes of a fiddle played by an old man who swayed with shut eyes, rapt in his discordant scraping.

In fact, the hotel was doing good business that night. The whirlpool, as a temperance tract might say, was a-booming and a-boiling, sucking down men's wages and perhaps their health; the boys were "on the tear," and the hotel resounded with their revelry. Those who had fallen lay splayed out upon the floor in drunken sleep;

those who were sick lay outside in the night. The scene reminded me a little of boating suppers and undergraduates; but the action, of course, was much more vigorous, as befitted grown-up men.

Now I had no idea of the arrangements usual in such places, in a loggers' hotel, and there was no one around to tell me. I quailed before the publicity of confronting the majestic bartender at his bar, and drawing the attention of a roomful to my ignorance.

I felt conspicuous, for by some accident I still wore a dirty collar. Men eyed me askance ... and it was some time before I took my courage in both hands and walked nervously into the kitchen. I asked timidly for a *bed* (a more tactful word I thought than *room*), and a bartender off duty took me up to the second storey—a great loft of a place under the sloping roof—and told me to hunt among the beds until I found what I wanted. "The beds up here are good and *clean*," he said, with friendly assurance (no lice, he meant). That was all I wanted to know. I realised the situation at once, found a fine clean space of floor beneath an open window, spread my blankets, and turned in.

Gentlemen were breathing stertorously from adjacent beds ... and the roar from beneath, and scraping of chairs and shuffling, and the busy hum from the bar, were as the noise of the sea—lulling me to sleep.

3 A.M.—I must have been in a heavy sleep. Bump! bang! bump, bump! wallop! smack!! A hubbub of talk on the floor beneath. "Albert! Albert!" cried a woman's voice, "come inside! come! come!" and more talk; and then a loud, angry voice—"That'll teach you to behave more decent for the future." Upstairs, some of us sat up in bed listening and wondering ... and soon in the light that shone up the staircase we saw the fat and solemn Dutchman mount slowly up the stairs and get into his bed—with ineffable dignity. He was insufficiently clad in a very short vest, that reached just below his armpits.

Next morning I heard the rest of the story: which I am afraid I must leave rather vague. The Dutchman, as it were, had been vague himself about the geography of the hotel ... and had walked into the proprietor's bedroom. The proprietor got up, and it was the noise the Dutchman's body made as it hit each stair that had awakened us. We laughed ourselves sick over it; but the Dutchman never turned a hair. What a curse self-consciousness would have been for him!

Hunger, next morning, drove me down to pay my fifty cents for breakfast and pass the wary sentry who held the eating-room door. Hunger appeased, I went into the public room. There I found a few pale, silent men who still continued at the card game of the night before. Some had won and some had lost, but the bar, I gathered, had taken all the money. A bartender was tidying up the room, putting in place the upturned chairs, and sweeping the rough surface of the floor that was all torn and splintered by the spikes of loggers' boots. Several men slept where they had fallen. The hotel was very quiet.

Outside the morning sun shone on a pretty scene: on the little bay, the warehouse raft, the boats upon the beach, the boats at anchor; on the ruffled blue waters of Western Channel, and on the forest slopes beyond. Round the hotel were desolate black stumps of trees and great litter and disorder of splintered planks and tree limbs, empty casks and straw and tin cans. Beyond this the half-burnt logs of the hotel clearing lay thick, criss-cross, where they had been felled; and then the untouched forest began.

I had a damaged foot, as I have said before, and there was no place where I could walk. For a man cannot get along the steep rocky shores in that country without going up, for long stretches, into the woods; and the woods, for walking in, are "something fierce," as persons say—underbrush and fallen logs, rocks and crevices, to hinder one; and needles of the devil-clubs to fray one's temper. There is no comfortable covering of soil to walk upon; moss and huge trees alike grow on the very rock, sustained by the heavy winter rainfall upon a scanty pretence of soil. So I did not dream of walking exercise, but sat myself down upon the hotel veranda and sat bored—my mind churning uselessly at plans of action that would not form.

About half-way through the long morning a bald-headed elderly man came out upon the veranda and stood near me, gazing listlessly at the sea and at the sunny hills beyond. He had been fighting, I supposed, for his eye was painfully discoloured, and a blood-stained handkerchief, that had been a bandage, hung loosely round his neck. "You bin hurt?" I asked by way of making talk. "You-betcher," he replied, "bin hit by the flying end of a broken wire rope." He seemed, now that he came to notice it, to take a mild interest in his injury. There was a horrible deep gash. I had a small box of medicines, and I cleaned the wound with an antiseptic and put a proper bandage on. The man's name was Al.

Now the getting of hot water from the kitchen for the cleaning of Al's eye made me acquainted with the hotel proprietor's wife, and my next move was obvious. There is always work around the house that a woman wants to have done for her. So after the midday meal I laid in wait. When my chance came, "Say! Mrs. Jones," I said, "you've got to find me a job. I'm just crazy-tired of setting around doing nuthin'." I had to overcome her astonishment that I should want to work for exercise and not for pay.

They gave me a saw and an axe, sledgehammer and wedges, and I spent a happy afternoon upon the hillside behind the hotel, sawing up a big log for stove wood. It felt good to be at work again, using one's muscles and sweating and feeling young. Sunday I worked also, early and late, and Monday and Tuesday morning— and I split an amazing big pile of wood. I began to get known. I was noticed at my morning swim—the first man, except the White Frenchman, ever known to enter willingly those chilly waters. Then logging gentlemen, between drinks, would wander up the hill to see the extraordinary person who liked to work and who worked for nothing. I used to throw my coat over a saw-cut that was not straight enough for the professional eye, and possibly seat myself, blushing, over unfinished axe work that I wished to keep private. For my vanity gets on the grill whenever I realise that I shall never become a decent axeman. I remain, in spite of bitter effort, a mere butcher of wood.

My patient, of the damaged eye, used to bring me up oranges and sit and watch me work. In confidence, he showed an oppressive regard for dramatic convention. "I made up that about the wire hitting me," he said; "it don't look decent for the folks to know how it was really done. It was a fist, or a corner of a table, or maybe someone's boot that hit my eye, sah. To tell the truth, I am ashamed to say I don't know which. We was all drunk, sah; and we were all ashamed of ourselves next morning."

I had to give him a dose or two of bromide, as he was getting shaky, from much whisky, and I feared the horrors might come. He quite agreed with me that he ought to go back to work, but.... Al must have come from the South, to judge by his courtly manners. "Yes, sah," he told me, "I'm quite the old-timer in these parts. I tend hook in these camps about here, sah. I lived three years with Fanny Brook, sah" (he mentioned it as you would a diploma), "down at Cape Mudge... I'm very sorry" (suddenly noticing the little nine-year-old niece of the hotel proprietor's); "I oughtn't to have said that... As for whisky, I'm afraid I'm a hopeless case, sah."

"Why did you quit Jenkins' camp?" I asked him.

"Well, you see, sah, it was a *professional* matter. I was tending hook there. Perhaps you know something about steam?... Well, I'll explain that for getting out logs a man must have 160 lbs. pressure. The engineer said he had, but I knew he was scared of the donkey-boiler and he only got 130 at most out of her. With that pressure I couldn't get out the logs, sah, in a satisfactory manner... Jenkins and I parted very friendly, sah... Yes, I was getting six dollars a day and board... Oh, well! what does it matter what wages a man like me gets, sah? I only drink them up." You may sniff and cry common sense; but it warms me to meet a man who has been capable of single-minded action for a simple sentiment. Here was Al, who had been asked to tolerate some mediocre doings—and his soul had rebelled, and he had left a comfortable job. I like this better than the trained sense for instantaneous compromise that many decent, educated men develop. I like the artist's pride, the boyish craving for *efficient* performance, the feeling for sound, clean work, and the very moderate care for consequences.

It is not easy for a stranger to make his way about this northern country, or find out what is going on. He has to "get acquainted" and learn the art of listening. This was brought home to me on the

Tuesday afternoon when I learned, by purest accident, in overhearing talk, that Carter's steamboat had been lying all this time at anchor in Port Browning, and that Carter's partner was expected back from town by the *Cassiar* that very night. Port Browning was but a few miles away. A man was going there to fetch the mail, and so I rolled my blankets and took them to the man's boat and held myself in readiness to start.

I had not done so badly at Hanson Island. True, I had been extravagant, eating three meals a day, and I had lost half a dollar and spent one modest dollar at the bar, six men and the barkeep sharing my invitation. But in the dining-room they had protested against my paying for my meals; and for the last two days had refused, blankly, to take my money; and so I had twelve dollars left.

Now that he heard I was about to leave, the hotel proprietor took me to the bar and, roll of bills in hand, asked how much he owed me for the wood that I had cut. He became very pressing, but I refused stoutly to take payment; an altruistic-looking act born of cold calculation on my part. So, over a friendly drink, he gave me advice and talk about the ways of the logging country; about employers and camps and the various troubles a man might have in getting his wages. "For," said he, "these boss loggers have their business affairs in a hopeless mess as a rule. Young man," he said impressively, "*always keep your money drawn up to date!*" I was to come to him again, he said, should I be out of work, for there were jobs for me in camps near by. And so I left the hotel with a comfortable feeling about the future and a zestful consciousness of my success as an advertiser.

Al escorted me to the boat. "Say," he said, "how are you fixed for dollars? Have you plenty of dollars? I insist that you should tell me if you're wanting any..." I had to assure him fervently that I was well fixed. But any time I want help I understand I am to apply to Al Hoskins. He is my friend and "don't know what to do for me." So you see what a little antiseptic dressing will do, at no expense of effort... The other man and I launched the boat, rowed down the channel and round into the lagoon, and reached the end of the land trail that goes to Port Browning.

# CHAPTER IV

# At Port Browning

T HERE IS A BIG dead cedar that overhangs the sea just where the land trail starts from the lagoon shore. Near this tree the other man and I made fast our boat. A number of other boats were already anchored there; their owners gone to get mail or small supplies at the Port Browning Store, or to get themselves drunk at the Port Browning Hotel. The other man hid the oars and rowlocks of our boat some way off in the woods, carefully. Then he took my bag, friendly-like, and carried it. I shouldered my pack and followed.

There was good walking on the trail; good footing and little climbing over fallen timber. The way wound up and down on small hillsides; past pools of water, past small bubbling creeks, past clearings where the slideways and the high stumps of big trees and the small shattered timber showed that the logger had been at work. But we took scant notice of such forest sights. My companion, who came originally from Tennessee, was deep in questions about Australia, a country which he thought he would much like to visit, by way of changing his present life. I was wholly disconcerted by the speed at which he walked and by the awkward stepping of my damaged foot. And this went on until we met two men, and stopped awhile to talk to them and take a drink of whisky, neat, out of their bottles.

"There's quite a dose of them down at the hotel," they said, and grinned, "just a-coming in from all parts . . . No, not drunk yet . . . about ten o'clock tonight—at least, that's the time we got drunk last

night. Where do they all come from? It's a wonder! . . . Well, boys,
we'll push on; we've got to get across the inlet tonight if the west
wind don't come up . . ."

Two miles of trail brought us to Browning Harbour, and then the
woods ceased and we came out upon a small clearing by the beach.
We passed tree stumps and rubbish piles, outhouses and a log-pen,
a meat-house and the shack where the proprietors and barkeeps
live, and came round the back of Port Browning Hotel to the
veranda and the barroom door.

It was "steamer night" — men had come in to meet the *Cassiar*
— and so the barroom was crowded full. Men sat all round the walls
on chairs and benches; men lined up across the strong breast-high
barricade of the bar, two ranks deep (someone was spending
money!). A fiddler worked, and another man gave an accompani-
ment of tom-tom by tapping on the fiddle-strings with chopsticks.
Within five minutes of my entry there arose a dispute that burst into
a sharp, sudden fight (and one man down), and a long, slow-subsid-
ing growl of argument afterwards. This was a mere incident in one
corner of the room. Altogether there was a pleasing, lively clack and
movement in the barroom scene; and everyone seemed happy. Outside the door there was a gentleman "coughing his toenails up" in
pangs of whisky sickness. But the drinking on the whole was very
moderate, and there was little to offend.

The noisiest man in the barroom was a hideous, great hulk of a
hobo from the States, an overgrown kid like the comic countryman
of the stage. "Look bad but feel good" was his motto, and certainly
his face did look horrid. I thought it was due to drink, and possibly
kidney trouble, but they tell me the man got into trouble one day
with one of the hotel proprietors. The hotel man took a chair and
laid him out, and while he lay upon the ground André the Frenchman came and jumped upon his face with spiked boots . . . and the
man lay there stunned and drunk and bleeding for hours. "Interfere? Well, I guess we was all drunk. Besides, we didn't know but
what André might have had something against him." A queer example of the apathy that sometimes falls upon a crowd of spectators.

Later in the day the hobo did a clog-dance, the floor being for the moment clear. "I'm a bob-cat with tousels in me ears," he howled and bawled. He was a nuisance. Little Jem, the bartender, lifted the flap of the bar, came quietly out, caught the hobo by the seat of his pants, and slung him out through the door. It was a great relief.

There were men in the bar-room who had been at Hanson Island and had seen me there. Some of them nodded to me and called out questions, and I began to feel more at home and less under critical observation. Of course one or two had probably sized me up as being strange; "splendidly educated," perhaps. Who knows? I may even have been held capable of keeping books — that crowning achievement of educated men. For although one's gait and dress and manners may pass muster, although one may even catch the intonation of voice and the cadence of swear-words and swear-phrases, yet one uses like a foreigner wrong words and expressions. "Yes, certainly!" is a queer way of saying "sure thing!" — to give a small example.

Accent and foreign speech make one conspicuous. I find it convenient to be as unobtrusive as I can be with comfort, whether I live in London or in Port Browning. An English air is new and queer to Western men who meet it for the first time. It is offensive to those who have met it before, and who have rankling suspicions of what it may (and too often does) imply — the conscious mental superiority the partly educated person carries with him. You have got to be straight if you want to make friends with men of less intellectual training than your own. Patronise the humbleness of a man's attainments in your heart, and he (if he is worth anything) will feel the falsity you conceal. Heavens! we see the second-rate in our own souls, and see it without emotion; tolerating such old habitual defect. And yet to see the same second-rate, the same limitation, in men of less active brains gives us excuse for conscious superiority. The moment we think we look downwards upon, and understand, the workings of another's mind we feel a mild contempt for him.

The logger cannot stand a missionary. It must be rather a dreadful thing to be a convinced missionary and to have to mix with your fellow men, not frankly (you and the others, just human beings together), but as a man exploiting the forms and even the spirit of friendliness for a more or less secret purpose of your own . . .

I enjoyed my evening in that barroom thoroughly. I liked "the boys." It was pleasant to see men of all ages active and light-hearted, unconscious of their years and of the future, free of the West. Many of them might be commonplace in nature; but the average of character seemed high, as averages go; and there were some fine, virile-looking men, decided personalities, amid the crowd. All the men were firm of flesh and weather-stained. And if whisky was their bane, better this, to my mind, than that dreary scheming to indulge in Comfort that meets one everywhere in city life.

# CHAPTER V

# At Carter's Camp

THE SCENE NOW SHIFTS to Carter's camp, where accident had played havoc. A log, hooked to the wire cable used for hauling, had broken loose upon the steep hillside, and charging down, had smashed into the donkey-engine and broken some of the machinery. Carter at once "shut down"—that is to say, he discharged all his men. I reached the camp the very day the men were paid off, and the steamboat *Sonora,* that had brought me up, turned round at once and took the whole crew down to Port Browning. The smashed machinery was sent to Vancouver for repairs. Carter and I were left alone at his camp at the head of Coola Inlet—seventy miles from anywhere. Carter had hired me, and I went to work.

Now there were about three hundred logs floating about inside the line of boomsticks that was stretched across the mouth of the little bay in which Carter had his camp. Carter decided to occupy himself, and me, in "rafting up" these logs — that is to say, in massing the logs together in a firm raft fit for a tug-boat to tow away to the sawmills down south. So we set to work to bore holes in the ends of long logs called boomsticks; and these boomsticks we chained together. This chain of logs we then anchored out to form a floating enclosure on the surface of the bay. The enclosure could open at one end.

The work, for a practised boom-man, was now to take a long, light pole, and jumping upon a floating log, to stand upon the log and pole it into the boomstick enclosure. This he would have to do with log after log until all had been poled inside and all lay tight together, parallel, in ranks, the width of the enclosure. Then he and his mates would have to chain this mass of logs across, solid, and so obtain a raft that would keep its oblong shape under the strains of movement and of towing.

The *practised* boom-man, alas, would do all this. Carter, for example, did. He went hopping from log to log, poling one here, one there; poling half a dozen at a time. He had worked upon the rivers "back East" in his youth, where logging men learn early to "ride a log." He had the perfect balance of a mountain goat, and the logs obeyed his will.

Now there are many men who never learn to ride a log, and at the best of times I should not for a moment pretend to be able to do so myself. So with a damaged foot I found myself, on Carter's boom, a figure of hopeless incompetence. I would jump upon a log, a good big steady log chosen on purpose. The log would begin to roll under my feet, as logs will. I would keep walking up and up; the log would roll faster and faster; soon I would be running up. Then my balance would begin to go and I would take a flying leap for any log that floated near — or else, splash! go headlong into icy water. The water was ice water from a glacier-fed stream.

Carter fished me out three times in one day, and there were times when I fell in and kept the fact to myself. For it was most mortifying that I should be making so futile a first appearance. Here I was working under the very eye of a new boss! I dreaded to think what disrepute might come upon my powers of work. I shuddered at the risk of that blighting verdict "He don't *know* nuthin'; he can't *do* nuthin'." Suppose that should be said behind my back as I have heard it said of other men. Vanity suffocated at the thought!

Other troubles I had too. My muscles had recently become soft from enforced disuse; my hands were soft; my power of muscular endurance had suffered woefully. And now I had to become acquainted again with that instrument of torture, the four-inch auger, that bores a hole a man can push his fist into. Oh, the back-breaking job of boring boomsticks when your auger keeps biting into stubborn knots! Oh, sore and puffy hands!

Carter had always work for me to do even when the tide was out and "rafting up" was interrupted. I could take the big cross-cut saw and saw off the shattered ends of logs that had shot violently upon the rocks of the sea-bottom when diving from their downhill run. I could split long billets of "cordwood" for fuel for future voyages of Carter's steamboat *Sonora*.

Besides all this I cooked our meals. About my cooking, of course, I was not shy; for like most other men I knew, in my heart, that I was the "finest kind" of cook—that I could "slap up a meal" with any man; and Carter would stand anything rather than cook himself.

So I was hard-worked enough, and happy too. For it is good to be at healthy work with clean Nature around you. There are worse occupations than working for wages in a camp.

I find that "working for wages" suits me well enough—suits me, that is (like any other work), for some period of my life on earth. If I have dry underclothes to start out in, and if my boots are not too much worn out, and if my hands and feet are warm, I can turn out at the standard hour of seven o'clock on any morning with a happy day ahead. There will be plenty of work to do, plenty of occupation for mind and body, plenty of soul-satisfaction. There is no need to bother oneself as to whether this thing or that thing is worth the doing, or whether it is going to be of real use or lead to anything or satisfy ultimate standards. The boss settles all that. He is a fellow-being who really *wants* certain things done, things essential to his happiness. He has private reasons for this, reasons beyond my interest or concern. The simple fact that here is a man who is really keen to have some rather interesting things done and wants me to join him at once in doing them—this makes a great appeal to me. It gives me a motive—an immediate simple object in life—for the time being. There is definite work to be done: Nature and natural obstacles to be struggled against (and not one's fellow men); and there is, besides, the vanity of not being seen to be incompetent. There is the great charm of life in uncivilised parts—what Higgs calls the "perpetual pleasure of small achievements"; the backing yourself to beat all sorts of difficulties by the ingenious use of the

few simple means you possess. Conditions and surroundings are so
varied and changeful that you are always dealing with something
new: you are the delighted amateur experimenting. Even if you get
stuck at a monotonous job — long spells of rowing, sawing and splitting cordwood, using pick and shovel, or breaking rocks with a
hammer — there is still the great pleasure of working up the *intensity of effort,* trying (vulgarly) to beat time, or to beat some other
man's performance, or simply to see how long your own endurance
will hold out; playing games with your work and with your own body
and character, as small children play with their food. Then, too,
there is the athletic and artistic pleasure in trying to develop effort-
less accuracy in the swinging of an axe, or in the delicate, light-
handed movement of the big saw. There is plenty of call upon your
physical endurance and upon your moral qualities. The needs and
sudden emergencies of the work, and the presence of other men's
standards of achievement right before your eyes, give you stimulus,
and check self-indulgence and the fatal sliding-down of feeble man
to ease and comfort. There is call upon your reasoning powers, too,
and upon your goodwill to help your fellow's work. You are made to
think over the commonplaces about education, and to realise that a
man can get well trained in his more generous character without
troubling the books very much. In days of depression, in days when
you do not like the job you have — still, by supper-time you will be
so many dollars to the good, dollars that are net profit. How much
net profit is there in many a genteel job in England? Take away the
necessary "expenses of the position," the cost of clothes, holidays,
and small amusements and sports (that avert decay and death!).
How much is left, net money profit?

And if my balance-sheet for the year is no great affair, in your
sophisticated eyes; if I spend, in idleness in bad winter weather or
in wandering to fresh fields of effort, much of my yearly profit; if, in
fact, my year's work has inevitable interruptions — still, is not the
best, most satisfying work work that is intermittent, that gives one
rest after toil, time for recuperation? Work such as that is a more
buoyant affair than the deadly treadmill work that goes on, soogey-
moogey, day in day out, for forty-nine perfunctory weeks of the year.

The "expenses of one's position" in a camp are working gloves and working boots, dungaree trousers that cost a dollar, underwear and shirts that you can patch or darn; and soap. You do not have to bother how you look, nor whether you live at a reputable address. As long as you do your work, nobody makes it his business to care a cent about the correctness of your demeanour or of your morals, or to dictate to you, impertinently, about your private affairs. You do not have to submit to anything — not even from public opinion. There is a toleration that surpasseth all the understanding of the old-country English.

If your work, or your boss, or your food, or your surroundings displease you, you can move at once elsewhere, provided times are reasonably good — as they usually are. And you have no dreary effort in the moving, nor mass of stuff to move. Just blankets rolled in your canvas, and a canvas bag stuffed with spare underclothes and socks and the other few things you do not throw away on the bunk-house floor.

Then you are not conscious, like the city man, of playing a small and most unimportant part in a gigantic scheme. You do not feel the egoism-depressing thought that if you do not do your little piece of work there are hundreds of better-qualified men of your profession waiting just behind your shoulder for the chance of grabbing it. Out in the woods there is more work than there are men to do it. If you do not do the piece of work you are asked to do, plainly there may be some hitch in getting it done. It may not get done at all. Your work *makes a difference.* Yourself and your decisions have some obvious *importance.* Life plays sweet tunes to soothe and make robust your egoism. You are vain of being yourself, and in this happy state money can clearly be regarded as a by-product.

Altogether there is much to make a man feel good — and he mostly does — at such healthy work. Then the dinner-gong booms from the cookhouse as a pleasant surprise; he goes down and eats heartily; sits awhile and yarns; shakes off the slight distaste that comes from muscular stiffness and cold, sweat-soaked clothes, and goes back and works with *visible result* till supper-time draws near and he begins to feel he has done about enough. After supper, lying on his bunk with his mind in a pleasant state of rest, he can feel secure that all the worries of the day are buried and done with forever. The day's work is over; it has been, as it were, a complete life. The new life of tomorrow is like the life beyond death — it and its problems can, remarkably well, wait their turn.

*Hand-loggers.*

# CHAPTER VI

# Dave and Speculation

I N BRITISH COLUMBIA, you should know, a man could go anywhere on unoccupied Crown lands, put in a corner post, compose a rough description of one square mile of forest measured from that post, and thus secure from the Government exclusive right to the timber on that square mile, subject to the payment of a rent of one hundred and forty dollars a year ("No Chinese or Japanese to be employed in working the timber"). Such a square mile of forest is known as a "timber claim."

Years ago the mill companies and the pulp-concession speculators secured great stretches for their future use — on nominal terms that rankle now in every logger's breast. But the woods, to ordinary men, seemed limitless. A logger might stake a claim or two over specially tempting timber if he intended, some time, to cut logs in that place; but why should he take up leases as a speculation? He felt that he might just as well lock up a coal mine, speculating on the future exhaustion of the world's coal supplies.

But during the last year or two, logs that in the northern country had been worth but three or three and a half dollars the thousand feet (board measure) had jumped to eight and nine and ten. The camps made "all kinds of money"; new camps sprung up like mushrooms. Donkey-engines could be got on credit, from the sawmill companies; supplies could be got on credit, from hopeful storekeepers. Hand-loggers were strung out along every fiord, along every island shore — putting in logs against Time. They could make

43

six and seven dollars a day per man, even on slopes that had been
hand-logged and re-hand-logged in days before the boom. Now a
ten-dollar price for logs had stimulated the demand for good logging
claims, and then suddenly it had dawned on everybody that such
claims were limited in number and were being taken up rapidly.
There had arisen a fierce rush to stake timber. Hundreds and hundreds of men—experienced loggers, inexperienced youths from
town—blossomed as "timber-cruisers." The woods were furrowed
with their trails. Men in rowboats and sailboats, and small, decrepit
steamboats, and gasoline motorboats had pervaded the waters of
every channel and fiord. They had staked the good timber, and then
the poor timber, and then places that looked as if they had timber
on them, and then places that lacked that appearance. What happened, in the end, to all these claims I do not know. They were sold
successfully, I believe, to vague "American interests," and to readers of advertisements in Chicago and Philadelphia and the East
generally. The catching of the English investor seems to be becoming less of a topical pleasantry in current talk; and so I suppose that
"fishing for suckers" has, nowadays, to be done nearer home.

I was meditating upon the glories of the recent boom (boom that was
then fading away but that had not yet disappeared) while working
one day alongside Carter on the raft. We two were taking a small
winch, that stood upon a floating platform, from point to point along
the raft's edge and hauling swifter sticks across from the far side,
over the mass of logs, and chaining these sticks, solid—to brace the
raft for towing. The raft was about four hundred feet long.

Suddenly Carter's keen eye saw smoke far down the Inlet, and
soon a small steamboat came into sight and made her slow way to
the usual anchorage where the tide flats begin, a mile below the
camp. Then there came a man rowing. He reached our raft, tied up
his boat, and came hopping over the logs toward us. It was Dave
Felton.

I liked the look of Dave Felton; it gave my eyes pleasure to see
him. He was a fine, tall, strapping young fellow, active in every
movement as a cat; with an open, healthy face, and an outward

bearing that made you imagine sound qualities within. In talk with him a breeze seemed to blow pleasantly upon you, a sort of bracing air full of Dave's firm belief in himself. People feel it. "There's a man who'll make money," they say, and nod to one another . . .

Dave was a great worker, one of the best of woodsmen; and he used to be a logger and run a small camp. But the boom in timber leases had fired his explosive brain, and for a year before we saw him then he had been "timber-cruiser." He had flown about in rowboat trips, had gone tearing through stretch after stretch of desperately encumbered forest, and had staked and staked, lease after lease, in a sort of frenzy of optimism that had proved irresistible even to purchasers in Vancouver. I expect Dave's leases were no worse than thousands of others that were staked about this time. I dare say it may pay to take the logs off them some day when timber gets scarce and wonderfully high in value. I know, anyway, that they were good enough for the dealers in Vancouver. Dave was a straightforward, give-you-a-square-deal sort of fellow. He assumed that these people must have good reasons of their own for wanting to buy timber leases. It was not his business to question or to doubt. He only knew that he had lived hard, laborious days and explored some frantically bad country to supply this mysterious want felt by "monied men" in Vancouver and "back East" — and that his work had paid. He reckoned that he had made some fifteen thousand dollars in the year. There "was a boom on" — that was all.

And now Dave had come up to talk business with my boss — my boss who had himself leases for sale, and could not sell them. We knocked off work at once and honoured the bottle that Dave had thoughtfully brought with him. Then we had supper, and after that we set the stove going in the bunkhouse and drew up documents. Mine was the pen. Then we finished the bottle and let ourselves go — in talk. We had a glorious evening.

It was not my gamble, and I was at liberty to feel older and wiser than Dave. The feeling was depressing, because Dave reminded me of my youthful enthusiasms. As I sat warming myself at that bunkhouse stove I watched him — and envied him. In comparison I felt myself worn-out; a poor relic of burnt-out energy. But as the evening passed my mood brightened. Dave just radiated heartiness. He paced restlessly up and down the creaking floor, his head among the clouds, where scheme after scheme coiled and revolved. He talked in an absorbed way, he looked at us with unseeing eyes; he was "just a-boiling" inwardly with energy and schemes. He grew breathless. We arrived at the stage of enthusiasm when all talk at the same time, our eyes opening to the marvellous opportunities that lay around us, resources of Nature that lay waiting for us to secure a monopoly upon them. We went late to bed.

Next morning I found myself alone at work. The little steam-boat's smoke had vanished soon after dawn, taking away Dave Felton. And as for Carter, he had had an inspiration overnight, and piling his blankets and a week's food into a boat, had gone upon a trip up-river to explore a place where he thought millions and millions of feet of timber might be awaiting the happy purchaser of timber leases.

So for several days I worked all by myself. I sawed blocks off the damaged ends of logs and split billets of wood—three feet, four feet, six feet long—for the steamboat's next trip. Now and then during the days I would hear the noise when the two hand-loggers across the Inlet would send a tree shooting down the mountain-side—a rumbling noise of thunder even at three miles or so. From down the coast would come at times the noise of chopping from where Mike Kendall, solitary man, worked by himself. But all these men were at bitter feud with Carter and never would approach his camp. So, except for an Indian gentleman who called in his canoe to try to trade his wife for whisky, I saw no one. Winter was coming on and the market for logs was somewhat glutted. Coola Inlet for fifty miles or so was bare of men. Only deserted shacks of hand-loggers remained . . .

Then Carter came back, and we two went to work upon the hillside near the camp. We sawed and split up cordwood, future fuel for the donkey-engine. And for several days our brains were seething with the prospectus of the Coola Inlet Pastoral Colony Syndicate, that was to embank and reclaim the wide stretches of grasslands on the river delta. Carter could not keep away from me. He had to talk or burst. He had returned from his trip dazed with possibilities. Every ten minutes he would come across to where I worked and discuss a fresh extension of our schemes; much to the hindering of my work. But in the evenings, more soberly, he put me to work upon "the books." You know the little thin pocket account-books dear to landladies and laundries. Imagine three or four of these chock-full with the store bills, the wage accounts, the gambling debts (one to another) of the dozens of men who had stopped at that camp, as it were a hotel, during the months of that year. Imagine all these accounts jotted down in smudgy pencil, by inapt fingers, at odd moments, from memory, in the desperate hurry of a work-weary, sleepy man. Imagine, entangled with these, the long sequence of accounts with hand-loggers who, from time to time, had drawn outfits and supplies from the camp on credit . . . Imagine me wrestling in this illegible jungle of words and figures with the awful complications of the accounts with P. François *and Co.*; P. François *personal*; François and Fisher; Fisher and Simpson (a change of partnership due to a quarrel); Fisher *personal*; Fisher guarantor for Simpson!!!

In the late evening when, weary of accounts, I would lie blissfully upon my bunk, Carter would sit and smoke, warming himself at the bunk-house stove and watching his clothes hung aloft to dry in the rising heat. Under these genial influences his stern mood would thaw and he would discourse about various things "a man might do to make money" — schemes that would bring to mind experiences of his past and suggest reveries and chains of thought. He would tell me of his life and give his views. I made a good listener. I used to wish to goodness that I could remember it all afterwards.

# CHAPTER VII

# Carter's Earlier Career

THE PLANK HOUSES of Carter's camp were built upon separate rafts—platforms of huge great logs that floated high upon the water, and that could be towed conveniently from one place to another. There was the bunkhouse—the house in which men slept; the cookhouse—that was kitchen and store-room and eating-room combined (with a compartment for the cook to sleep in); and the office house where Carter slept when many men were in the bunkhouse, and where his business papers lay scattered on the floor. On the same raft as the office was the blacksmith's shop. The three rafts were moored together at a convenient place within the protection of the boom, making a little hamlet on the sea—primitive lake-dwellings, as it were.

One evening I came into the bunkhouse feeling very sleepy, and I took my boots off and put on dry clothing for the morrow (oh, luxury!), and rolled into my blankets in my bunk without delay. But Carter, it seemed, was feeling talkative; and talk he would, and have me listen. So I would doze awhile, and then his voice would rouse me into wakefulness; to feel the gentle heaving of the bunkhouse on the swell; to see the lamplight flickering on clothes hung up to dry, on rows of empty bunks, on Carter's pensive figure by the glowing stove, on socks and old boots and torn playing-cards that lay littered upon the floor. I would listen awhile to what the man said, and then I would doze again. Sorry I was afterwards that I did not keep awake. For Carter was telling me the history of his life.

I can remember, half-way through the yarn, the droning voice saying: ". . . and when I got to Seattle it was early morning. I walked round the streets looking for a bank, and pretty soon I found one — 'Miner's Exchange' it had written up over it, and a card hung in the window with 'highest prices paid for gold dust' on it. Not that I had any dust. My eighteen hundred dollars was all in bills in my pocket-book. Them bills made a nice little wad, I can tell you. I kept them in my hip-pocket. There was a feller standing on the edge of the pavement, and while I was waiting for the bank to open I got into conversation with him. There was a saloon a few doors down the street, and pretty soon I asked the fellow to come and have a drink. We had one, and I pulled out my pocket-book and got a bill out to pay for the drinks. Most of the change I put back in the pocket-book.

"Then two other fellers came in, and we got talking, and pretty soon we lined up to the bar for a drink or two. Them other fellers paid. By this time I saw that the bank would be opening, so I went out of the saloon and down the street and into the bank. I sez to the cashier, 'Make me out the forms, I want to deposit seventeen hundred dollars with you.' He sez, 'All right, hand her over'; and I put my hand to my hip-pocket to get the money. Holy Mackinaw! but you oughter have seen me jump: the pocket-book and the wad of bills was clean plumb gone!"

I must have dozed off: the slam of the stove door woke me. Carter had been putting in some wood. He was still talking.

". . . and soon I got into a ranching country. Sometimes I was refused, for there was too many hobos begging their way round them parts: sometimes I got a meal. Once I remember I'd had a meal, and as I went away, feeling cheerful, I picked up a stone and threw it — and hit an old duck and killed it. I picked up the duck and walked away. The old lady was watching me from the door, but she never said nothing. That duck tasted pretty good to me next time I made camp, too. You bet I kept a good look out for chickens after that.

"I'd been having a run of bad luck when I struck a little town where there was a branch railway line forking off in the direction I wanted to go. I started out from the depot, meaning to walk along the track as long as that railway kept going my way: but when I'd gone a hundred yards or so a new idea came into my head. There was a big Swede foreman working by the side of the track, and just beyond him was his gang — all Swedes.

" 'When's the next train going this way?' sez I.

"That foreman never showed he heard.

" 'Say, mister!' sez I, 'when does the next train start?'

"He went on working.

" 'D'you hear me?' sez I, soft-like.

"He went on working.

"I'd had no food for two days, and I tell you I was a desperate man. I noticed the Swede had the side of his head towards me, and I pulled back and let him have one — just back o' the ear. I thought for sure that gang of Swedes would have piled in on me with their picks and shovels: but they only stood and stared. The big fellow got up off the ground after a while and stared at me.

" 'When's that train go?' sez I. He told me.

" 'Gimme something t'eat,' sez I. He pointed to the depot, where his dinner pail was laying on a pile of ties.

" 'Not much,' sez I; 'they'll say I'm stealing it. You come along and watch me eat.' He done that. There was cold beef and potatoes and pickles and good bread in that dinner pail. I ate hearty . . .

" . . . and then I got footsore and threw away my blankets. Then I came to a town in the mountains where the houses was built on a side hill. The doors of the houses was on a level with the street; on the downhill side there were cellars built under the houses. The women useter keep their pies and kitchen truck in the cellars.

"I useter walk right into a cellar, collar a pie, and take it out, and anyone seeing me would think I was living in that house. A man wants to *look right* and have confidence and no one will bother him . . . And then I struck a job. You bet I froze on to that job. My nerve was all shaken, and I reckoned I would stick to that job for the rest of my life, never take no more chances of being broke in that blank-blank Chinaman's country. I held that rotten job for five or six weeks. Then I went out on the mountain making square timber by contract . . ."

I wish I had the materials for a life of Carter from the time when, as a boy of sixteen, he revolted against the grinding monotony of the little farm in Nova Scotia, to the present day, when, as Carter of Carter & Allen, loggers, Coola Inlet, his wanderings have (for the moment) ceased.

I've heard him tell of the long hours of work in eastern logging camps. "Men was plentiful and wages was terrible poor in them days. The bosses knew they had power over us; and they was hard, bitter hard. Being but a boy, I had trouble to stand up to the work. I useter fall into my bunk after supper, and the men would let me sleep there to the very last minute in the morning . . ."

He knocked around the camps in the Ottawa, and drifted over the border and worked on rivers in Michigan. Later in life he appeared as a trapper up in the Cariboo. It was on his return from there that his savings were stolen from him in Seattle. Hard times were on just then, and Carter, penniless, tramped for hundreds of miles before he found a job. I should judge that those were the hard times of 1893.

A year or two after this episode he was assistant timberman in a mine somewhere in Montana. This was his account: "It was a good camp; there was a number of mines and quite a little town. Saloons and stores done a good business there, and many of the men had wives and families. I was getting good wages, and I useter blow 'em in regular in the saloons and dance-houses along with the boys, having a hot time. I never had a cent to my name, and most times I was in debt to the saloon-keepers.

"One day I met a friend of mine on the street, and he was needing twenty dollars the worst way: he asked me for it. 'Boy,' sez I, 'I ain't got no money, but my credit's as good as money. Just wait a minute while I go and get the twenty from Jim O'Halloran.'

"Jim O'Halloran was a saloon man: many's the cheque I had blown in at his bar. I opened the swing door of the saloon, and there was O'Halloran talking with one or two men. 'Jim,' sez I, 'just lemme have a twenty, will you?'

"You'll hardly believe it, but that son of a —— began to excuse himself, pretending he was short of money himself. I was considerable put out, him doing that in front of them other fellers too; but I pulled meself together, seeing how it was, and I passed it off as if I hadn't noticed nuthin'. That was a lesson to me. I saved my next month's wages, and I had a haircut and shave, and bought a fine new suit of clothes and good boots and a new hat. Then I went and walked in the street, and hung around casual-like near O'Halloran's saloon. I useter do this every evening, and everybody would see me there and mention it in talk, and O'Halloran would worry, knowing he'd lost a good few dollars a month from me. He spoke to me once or twice, asking me to come and drink with him, and I was soft and friendly with him and called him by his given name. But I made that blank-blank whisky shark feel sick and kick himself for what he'd done . . . That gave me a start, and I quit drinking and went to live at a respectable boarding house kept by a widow lady.

"The women have a weakness for dark men—at least that's my experience—and me being a younger man in them days, with me black beard and black eyes, and me good clothes, and spruced up, I tell you I got on all right. Now that I'd quit the drink I had nothing to do after working hours, and I had lots of spare time. There was three women. One was a waitress at the restaurant where I useter eat. Another was a woman who ran a laundry—a fat lady she was. Then there was the widow who kept the boarding house. She didn't want me to pay for my board, but I wouldn't stand for that—I'm not the man to be beholden to a woman. It's a fine woman she was, that widow. I don't know but what I oughter have married that woman if I'd had any sense. It's kind of cheerful for a man to come home from work and find the shack all tidied up, and a fire burning, and supper all ready cooked, and someone to wash his clothes and look after him. Here I am, working day in and day out, wearing my heart out getting out logs, and what am I doing it for? I tell you, boy, work sometimes seems a terrible old thing to me.

"Well, the feller that was boss timberman over me got hurt, and the superintendent made me boss in his place. I began to quit spending my money on the women, and put me wages in the bank, saving them. Most of the men I knew was always short of money. I had money and I useter lend it, getting ten per cent a month. The men was drawing regular wages, and I tell you I made money, and there was damn few ever made a bad debt with me or got ahead of *me* any way.

"I kind of got tired of that town and the people, and when I had 2500 dollars saved up I left the place and came down to the coast. I'd heard an old fellow talk of the Cassiar country, and of how there was a big country that had never been prospected away up above the canyons on the Stickeen River. There's fine gold on all the bars on the lower Stickeen . . ."

That was a queer coincidence. I used to live up in Cassiar myself, and I remember talk of some man who came up to Telegraph Creek (where river navigation from the coast ceases) and hired Frank Calbraith and a mule train to pack his outfit away over the mountains to hell and gone up the Stickeen. The man stayed in there by himself, trapping and prospecting, and came out to Telegraph about nine months later with a few skins rolled up in his blankets and a great desire to talk to people. He had no gold, and the samples of rock he brought out proved to be valueless, on assay. The man was Carter!

"Say, boy, but I was glad to see that blank-blank collection of saloons. For a day or two Telegraph seemed to me the finest place on earth. Then I got a Siwash to take me down the river to Fort Wrangell in Alaska. Wrangell is not much of a place; mostly storekeepers competing for the Indian trade; they fair deafen a man with the row their phonographs make. I had to wait some days for the steamer, meaning to go down to Seattle and stay on the American side awhile. That's how I got acquainted with a fellow that was thinking of buying a sloop and going prospecting among the coast islands, down the mainland southwards: only he had no money. I had some money, and the sloop looked pretty good to me; she had been built for a real-estate man in Vancouver, a monied man who wanted to go out cruising on his holidays. That was a long time ago, and she was pretty old. We got her for 350 dollars; that was a big price. That's how me and the other fellow, Campbell his name was, came to go slooping. We was nigh a year on that sloop. There's not a channel nor an inlet nor an island on that coast I ain't visited. We prospected some, and fished some (for a cannery near the Skeena), and we kept ourselves in meat, hunting, and got a little fur, trapping. Yes. I'll tell you this talk about a man thinking himself above selling whisky to the Siwashes is just hot air. Give a man a chance and see what he'll do if he thinks it safe. Of course I know it's a pretty dam risky proposition most places when there's a policeman within a hundred miles of you: but there's places on this coast that are pretty far away from the police.

"Well, at last we anchored in Vancouver harbour. Holy, suffering Moses, but I was sick and tired of that blank-blank sloop!

"I packed up my stuff and threw it out on the wharf, and went up town to Billy Jones's hotel. Campbell went to a dealer and sold the fur that we had; he met me in the street and give me half the money. 'What you going to do about the sloop?' sez he. 'The sloop!' sez I; 'to h—ll with the sloop!! You can take that blank-blank birdcage and stuff it up a drainpipe for what I care. No more sloop for me this life.' I never seed Campbell again; I heard he sold the sloop to some Japanese . . ."

*Where hand-loggers once worked.*

# CHAPTER VIII

# Carter as Railroad Foreman

THE SLOOP TRIP and the subsequent drunk he went on in Vancouver left Carter bare to the world. I think it was then that he got a job as foreman of a pick-and-shovel gang on railroad construction. Carter in his time has held various jobs as foreman. But as a railroad foreman, a very despot, his ruthless energy and callous disregard of others must have made him immense.

I have never done labouring work on a railroad myself, but they tell me these railroad foremen treat their men like dogs, as the saying is; the men being, for the most part, Galicians and Polacks and Dagoes and such-like that cannot stand up for themselves. I do not suppose there is much physical violence; but I should imagine a railroad labourer is liable to treatment like that a private of the line may sometimes get from an evil-minded sergeant who finds vent for bad temper amid the opportunities of oppression that active service gives.

I remember Bob Doherty telling me of an experience of his. He had become "broke" in San Francisco. "The railroads was advertising for men at the time," said Bob, "so me and two other fellows went to the employment office and hired on. They gave us the usual free passes to the camp out on the line where we was to work. At least these here passes are not quite free. You have to hand over your bundle, and you don't see it again till you reach the camp you're booked for. The railroad people take your bundle as a sort of security to prevent you from running a bluff on them for a free ride to some other place you may be wanting to get to. If that's what you're after you can buy an imitation bundle specially made for the purpose at some of them little stores that's always to be found near a railway depot. The usual price is about a dollar.

"Well, I was telling you about our trip from 'Frisco. Me and the other two fellows reached a railroad camp; in good faith, for we wanted work of any kind. We went and spoke to a big foreman there, and he fetched out some shovels for us, and handed us each one. Holy Mackinaw! you just ought to have seen the way he gave us them shovels. He shoved them at us, rough-like, giving us a look same as if he was kicking us. Then he poked his face forward. 'Now then, you men,' he said, threatening, 'I'll have you understand that you're here to work, and work good; and I'm going to see you do. Get a move on right now, and move lively or there'll be trouble.' Gee! it fairly took our breath away. We looked at that foreman, stupid-like; and then we looked at each other. Then we took a tumble to the way things was in that camp, and we dropped our shovels where we stood and walked away. The foreman stood and stared at us and watched us go. He must have done some quick thinking, for he never opened his head to say a single word. I guess he didn't like the looks of us; maybe he hadn't come across no loggers not before."

From his work as railroad foreman, most probably, Carter got that manner and tone of voice of his—the manner and voice that have caused him so much trouble in this logging country and helped to make him so hated. I do not think he means it to happen, but once in a while, when he forgets himself in extra bad temper, he will show a trace of the old manner, and a tone will creep into his voice that will cause the man he speaks to to drop his tools and quit right there, and burn with a blind hatred for days after.

It is the tone that does it; the words he uses are altogether void of offence—there is nothing much to take hold of in what he says: nothing to provoke a fight. For Carter does not take the least interest in fighting; he has not the physical instinct—or else perhaps it is his morbid vanity that makes him shy of violence. I think he feels (what is the truth) that in this country it is an awful chancy business to expose his god—his quivering-sensitive picture of himself—to any risk by battle. You never know, if you are rash in quarrel, among loggers, but that your ordinary-looking adversary may not prove a sudden nasty thing in fighting-men, and be your better. It would nigh break Carter's heart should anyone lick him — and the fact be known.

Of course, out West, as elsewhere in the world, men do not readily come to blows. You will not see a fight from one year's end to another — among sober men; except those conjured up in mind by the short-story writer and the West-describing novelist. Why, for example, should sober loggers fight? Most loggers are easy-going; easy to get on with; men who have knocked about the Western world and have been taught, by experience, to be tolerant and passively considerate for others. They are not irritable and querulous; they put up with disagreeable things, that seem difficult to avoid, with philosophic common sense.

So in Western camps there are a most peaceable class of men. You may have many a dispute, "chewing the rag" about something, or even have a personal quarrel (though such are rare), without the affair going beyond words and noise.

Carter can go farther than most men in rough and insult-conveying quarrel talk which yet avoids the point where blows become inevitable. Outpointing a man in talk, however, is no great matter. Carter longs to wreak spite on a man with unseen hands. He would be soft and catlike, and let the hated man realise of himself, when too late, that Carter had contrived to "serve him dirt."

The spice of revenge is to *make men feel your power*. Carter is not very clever in carrying out these ideas: but he does his best.

Well, Carter was a railroad foreman and he made money. About that time there was a mining boom breaking out somewhere in the Kootenay country. Things looked pretty good there, and the newspapers were full of it. Carter figured that a boom is generally worth following; so he quit railroading, collected his savings, and started a hotel in one of the mushroom "towns" with which the very rumour of a boom will spot a country.

# CHAPTER IX

# Carter as Saloon Man

THE SALOON-KEEPER of the West, in places where more than one saloon exists, must work at an art that is no easy one. He must advertise, compete against the other whisky men; and yet there are no simple business means for doing this.

To begin with, there is practically nothing that he can do with the liquor supply except, of course, by varying the adulterants. All saloons have the same stock—the same whiskies and rums and port-wines and beers. There is absolutely no demand or support for anything new in the liquor line.

Again, it would be utterly useless to try cutting prices; for the standard price of drinks is two for the quarter-dollar—except in far-away districts like Cassiar or the Yukon. In the careless West, where, outside the towns and settled districts, the change for a quarter is a thing few men are conscious of, no one would care were the saloon man to charge a little less for drinks—playing games with such dust of currency as five or ten cent pieces. So it comes to this, that the pushful saloon man must try to increase his profits by making *himself*, his own person, popular. He must "make up" a little in the generous emotions, and pose just a little in the public sight; and yet show his transfigured personality in such wise that you would swear there was no limelight turned on it. I hate to mention these stage directions, because the saloon man when you meet him is usually so calmly and transparently himself—easy and yet professional.

There are two problems always before the perfect saloon man—
in the logging country, anyway. One is to convince men that he is a
good fellow and a good friend to each of them; the other, to make
them feel that he is a hard-headed business man whose shrewdness
cannot be imposed upon. To be a good fellow you must be seen to
have fine stock of generous feelings (that is your stock-in-trade); you
must be open and free, with a touch of the magnificent. Such qualities show up wonderfully fine under the bar lamps, against a gleaming background of plate-glass and bottles. They inspire men on the
other side of the bar to be chivalrous and free with their money.

Your reputation with the boys will cost you money to keep up.
You must at times be prodigal, ladle out free liquor suddenly, and
make episodes in men's memories. Your bartender, of course,
attends to the ordinary free drink that is part hospitality, part
ground-bait. But the serious expense lies in the credit that you must
give and in the many bad debts that you must incur. You will have to
lend some of the boys money when they are broke, and help some of
them out of awkward situations—and this sort of thing demands a
lot of judgment and a great knowledge of your men. The finance of
it, too, is difficult, especially as you have to carry so much in your
memory. Keeping accounts on paper is a dreadful strain upon your
capacity.

Life of worry! To know when to be generous and when to refuse!
And you must not show too generous, you must not show too
shrewd. You must walk a narrow, difficult path . . .

To educated persons glancing into the saloon world, the quiet-
eyed, blue-jowled, genial-shrewd brotherhood of barkeeps and proprietors may have a sinister air; sinister as a solicitor at his desk—at
your service, or as a surgeon just about to name his operation fee.
I make the comparisons deliberately, flicking at your respect for the
financial positions of prosperous lawyers and surgeons; for it annoys
me to feel your easy, educated contempt for saloon-keeping men
who have but slight control over the system under which they earn
their living. Lawyers and surgeons must sometimes steel their
hearts and take money from people in necessity and, like the saloon
man, strip a fellow-being bare; fortifying themselves with common

sense and coming down to reality from sentimental heights. I can remember the utter logic with which a surgeon once took my last borrowed dollar. There were, he pointed out, the running expenses of his position, the pressure of competition, the need to achieve a certain standard of comfort that he had set himself. And then, of course, there was the necessity of regaining the capital that he had sunk in his education, in gaining experience. The hotel man has the same need to use steel tentacles.

On the whole, the good-fellowship atmosphere of a loggers' saloon seems to supply some of the same sentimental food as the music, books, and stage-plays and other emotional influences with which the educated man nourishes (and too often satisfies) his sentimental nature. Here and there a barkeep, as here and there (let us say) an Oxford man, will prove capable of active kindliness.

What a fine flavour of the Tammany ward-politician there must have been about Carter in his saloon! Suave and easy, blarneying and intimate, lounging in white shirtsleeves, decently clothed in black! This I imagine would be his style when in good temper from success. But I do not think Carter would have proved himself, in the long run, a successful saloon man. He is always so earnest, so thorough, in his work, that he would never have been satisfied to make moderate efforts. He would have been too impatient to get men's money. The fell purpose of the whisky seller would have shown through too plainly; the boys would have become too conscious of it. And any little check to his plans, or disagreement with anyone, would have brought to light that desperate, drive-her-under pig-headedness and that bitter philosophy of life that Carter hugs to his soul. And no popularity could have survived that exposure.

Carter's career as a hotel man was, however, put an end to by other things. The bottom fell out of the mining boom, the towns decayed as fast as they had grown, and the day came when Carter rolled his blankets and walked out of his hotel, leaving all standing—for the weather and Time to dispose of. He was broke again, but Fate could not take away the past; and Carter had for ever the memory of "the time when I was running a hotel."

# CHAPTER X

# Carter the Hand-Logger

THE NEXT GLIMPSE into Carter's history I owe to Dan Macdonnell.

"The first time I ever seed Carter," Dan said to me one day, "was in a camp on Puget Sound where I was blacksmith. Carter comed and worked in the camp — just the same Carter that he is now — a desperate man to work, surly, and wanting to do everything according to his own ideas; thinking he could handle any job whatever in the woods, and show men who had worked all their lives at that job the right way to do it, whereas he can't do no more than butt his way through after a fashion. He used to be a nuisance to work with unless a feller let him have all his own way. I know the boss at that camp had to hold himself in all the time, to keep from losing his temper and firing Carter. But he felt there was no sense in losing a good worker like him. That was why Carter was able to stay so long with us.

"Before he came to our camp Carter had put in a few weeks lying round Seattle; drunk most of the time, but still hearing a good deal of talk. He had come across some men that had been up among the islands and inlets on the B.C. coast. They told him there was a growing demand for logs on the Canadian side, and that men were able to go up north 'most anywhere and make good money hand-logging. Carter got bitten with the idea of going up there himself.

"He was always brooding over the proposition, and whenever he'd get the chance he'd talk to us boys about it: what a fine show there was for a couple of men to go to Alert Bay and hand-log somewhere round them parts; and what big money they could make; and how they would be their own boss. You bet it was just poison for Carter to be doing work for another man.

"Then Carter would pick on some man or other and try hard to get him to go north, in partnership. He was after me one time. Now I was sort of willing to make a trip up and give the hand-logging a trial; not that I knew the first thing about it, but from what I could hear a man would soon get used to the work. But you wouldn't have caught me going as Carter's partner. Being partners with him means obeying him and being his slave; a man of any independence couldn't stay with him five minutes. Carter's as pig-headed as they make them; and wicked. Everything's got to be done his way; your way is wrong, and he won't even listen to what you are going to propose; and he'll go against your interests, and against his own, and wreck his whole business rather than admit himself in the wrong. You can't begin to argue with him; he flies off the handle soon as you open your mouth. I've no use for a man that goes on like that. Well, he couldn't persuade *me* to go with him, but he got hold of another feller, and soon after that Bill Allen made up his mind to join them. The three men saved up their wages for some time, and then they all quit the camp and went down to Seattle to take one of the Alaskan steamers that was used to stop at Alert Bay, going north. Carter had two hundred dollars saved up, and Bill had about five hundred. The other feller got drunk and missed the steamer, and they never saw him again."

And so, through Dan Macdonnell's eyes, you see Carter and Allen reaching the little settlement of Alert Bay and making their entry into the northern logging world — about five years ago.

One gets quaintly differing views of the past at times, out West. I can remember, for example, how our steamer going north at the time of the Klondike excitement put into that self-same Alert Bay; and how we, impatient passengers, spent an hour or so ashore, walking the new wharf, looking at the half-dozen new board-houses and the store. That commonplace modern scene remains fresh in memory; it was only ten years ago that I saw it — *only the other day,* as it were.

Yet, a year ago, I came to Port Browning and found a district of islands and inlets firmly occupied, in appearance, by man: camps scattered through it; steamers running directly to it; machinery at work; hotels and stores at business — everything old-established. And an old-timer told me, by an effort of memory, of a dim past before all this was; and in the remoteness of that period he mentioned Alert Bay — Alert Bay, forgotten of loggers, away over across the Straits; from where the first men came to hand-log round Broughton Island and the Inlets. And that dim past, if you please, was *only seven years ago*... It seems that the Siwashes showed resentment at the coming of the first few hand-loggers; in those far-away days. I remember Johnny Hill telling us a yarn about his first camp on Coola Inlet. He was building a cabin, working all alone: his partner a week's journey away, getting supplies. The Indians came to the cabin and actually tried to scare Johnny; a rather venturesome thing for modern Siwashes to give their thoughts to, yet one that hardly pleased a solitary man. Johnny went to the trouble of proving his title to the timber where he wished to work; a title acquired by impressive purchase, he told them, from the policeman at Alert Bay; a Government document that Johnny had steamed off a tobacco caddy, carefully; what you and I might call a revenue stamp. A trivial affair, but one that shows how *fresh* and free from white men the district must have been then.

At the time when Carter and Allen came north, Alert Bay was still the nearest jumping-off place for the Broughton Island district. There was a big store there full of all necessaries, for Indians and white fishermen and prospectors and trappers and such-like men. Twenty or thirty hand-loggers, I believe, also drew supplies from that store; and hand-logging tools could be bought there, at exorbitant prices.

So you can imagine Carter and Allen engaged in buying an outfit, and paying high for it. First they would get an eighteen-foot rowboat, with a good sail. Then tools: two heavy jack-screws, a light ratchet screw, big seven-foot saws, axes, heavy chains for chaining logs together, and many other things. Then flour and beans and bacon and the like in neat fifty-pound sacks, sewn up with oil-cloth; and tobacco in boxes; and a good-sized sheet-iron stove (with an oven up the chimney); and lots of matches (in that wet country) in tins; and maybe ammunition and a rifle. I bet Carter bought no fancy canned stuff, nor canned meats, nor any such rubbish; but he would have done himself well in cream and milk and syrup and little things a man really needs. And before the outfit was all stacked on the wharf Carter would have spent some five or six hundred dollars, cash down.

The talk at Alert Bay decided Carter and Allen to go search for a hand-logging proposition in the channels round Broughton Island. You can, if you like, picture the boat trips: the overladen boat; sailing winds; head winds; rough water; wetted cargoes; long, weary hours of rowing; runs for shelter behind islands; camps made in the dark by exhausted men. No men would spare themselves less than these two; no weather except the really dangerous would stop them. There was some queer anecdote about their power of endurance that I wish I could remember. But all I know is that they brought their stuff to the north end of Gilford Island, and "cached" it there, and started out with unencumbered boat to seek and choose a place where they should set to work.

In those days good timber was plentiful — good timber, on sea-coast slopes, that could be felled and shot right down to water — hand-loggers' timber. The country bristled with opportunities, for loggers; opportunities that were the making of men who had the spirit to venture out and seize them — men like Carter; opportunities that were then new-born of changed conditions in the lumber trade. Bitter to the Westerner are the mistakes of caution.

Many a man I have heard lament those days. "Boys, oh boys!" one would say, "why was we all so slow in coming to this country? We'd heard talk of it, and yet we held back: pess simmists, that's what we were. Men like Carter got ahead of us: had us all beaten. Why, anywhere round here all up the Inlets and round the islands there were the finest kinds of hand-logging shows. Why! the country *hadn't been touched!* There's men working today on places that have been hand-logged, and re-hand-logged and re-re-hand-logged since them days . . ."

So Carter and Allen had no need to cruise far around the shores of Broughton Island. They saw a boom or two hung out in little bays that opened from the channels; they received welcome at the cabins of the few hand-loggers already working there; but soon they rowed their boat past untouched forest slopes and knew that they had pushed ahead of the advance of man and human work. Everywhere their eyes were gladdened with the sight of timber handy to the beach; fine big cedars for the most part. Many trees they noticed, pointing sudden fingers, would drop right into water from the stumps when felled; a thought that made their hearts feel light. For "stumpers" are the most profitable trees that hand-loggers can hope to get; they need so little time and work.

So the two men looked eagerly for a small bay where wind and waves could not blow in with any violence; and this they had to choose most carefully, by observation of the signs of weather on the beach and on the trees: and by argument. What would the west wind do in summer? How would the north winds strike? Which way would the sou'-easter blow from off the mountains?

They found a bay that seemed to them secure from wind and sea, that lay close to a fine stretch of cedar forest. The hillside, too, rose from the sea at the right sort of angle; neither too steep for men to climb, carrying their tools, nor too flat for logs to slide down easily. A little creek fell with pleasant noise over the steep rocky beach of their little bay, and the two men found just by its bank a small flat place on which to build their cabin. So they pitched a tent, near to the shore, and by that act secured (by logger's courtesy) their title to the bay and to the neighbouring slopes. Then they made laborious rowboat trips, bringing their outfit up from where they had it hidden. That done, they set to work to make their camp. They did not build the ordinary log house, cedar was so plentiful. Instead, they cut a cedar log into eight- and twelve-foot lengths, and split the straight-grained wood into planks with their axes; and made a house-frame out of poles, and sheathed the frame with their cedar planks. Then they put in a floor of rough-hewn slabs; and fixed up bunks, and made a table, and set their cook-stove and its stovepipe in position. Outside the house they cleared a little flat; and under-neath a shed they set their grindstone; and made a stand where they could sharpen their big falling saws. Their camp was soon completed. Morning and evening blue smoke ascended from it, and marked its site against the mountain slope; and the sun shining sent a home-like gleam from yellow roofs seawards through the foliage.

Now the two men took their tools along the hillside to where tall, slender fir trees stood. These they felled into the sea, and cut a long sixty-foot log from each. They bored holes through each end of every log and chained the logs one to the other. So they had a long chain of logs to stretch across the mouth of their little bay. Anchored firmly to the shore on either side, that floating line of logs would give them harbour for the logs they meant to cut: once placed inside, no log could wander off to sea. Their "boom" (in loggers' speech) was "hung." They were now ready to start hand-logging.

"We worked right straight along when we were hand-logging; none of this here laying off for rain or blank-blank laziness. We made big money," was all I ever got from Carter concerning this period of his career. And yet romance lurks there. For the things men do in company are, after all, the easy things. What is so easy as to play one's part in charges on a battlefield; to join a crowd in doing certain work; to add your little mite to the pile your fellow workers make in sight of you? I find it impressive, I feel how much it is above the reach of average men, when men go out alone, or two or three together, against Nature in its wilderness; and there achieve noteworthy things by strain and stress of sweaty labour, hard endurance, laborious ingenuity. They work there, their own conscience driving them, with no crowd of fellow men to notice what they do. They have no helpful standards of conduct held before them; they are free to stand or fall by their own characters, that lack the supporting stays in which the morals of the citizen of towns live laced. And yet such men as Carter will "work right straight along" in dismal wet discomfort, in far solitary work, handling with imperfect tools enormous weights and masses—at mercy of callous, disaster-dealing Nature—undismayed.

# CHAPTER XI

# From Working-Man to Boss

C ARTER MADE GOOD money hand-logging. I have heard men tell of the desperate intensity with which he and Allen used to work; day in, day out; in wet and snow and shine. The first morning light would see them already at their place of work, perhaps a mile's rowboat journey from their home. There they would slave all day; carrying their sharp, awkward tools up through the hillside underbrush; chopping and sawing, felling big timber; cutting up logs, barking them; using their heavy jack-screws to coax logs downhill to the sea. At evening, tide serving, they would tow such logs as they had floated round to where their boom was hung, and put the logs inside, in safety. Then they could go home and dry their clothes, and cook supper, and sleep like dead men. Now this waiting on the tides, this robbery of precious hours of the work-sacred day, this towing (with a rowboat) of sluggard, slow-moving logs, racked Carter's soul and set him scheming. When he and Allen sold their first boom to a Vancouver sawmill he felt his chance had come. He bought the steamer *Sea Otter* for eight hundred dollars down. That ran him short of cash, and the short-sighted storekeeper at Alert Bay at once refused him credit. Even to this day that bitter, unexpected stab has left a scar on Carter's mind; and I know, the case arising, Carter would gloat to see that storekeeper drowning before his eyes — and taunt him as he sank. Carter never forgets, or forgives.

Bill Allen had to go to town and use his popularity to get an introduction to a storekeeper; a thing that Carter knew he could not do himself. So the crisis was tided over. They got supplies on credit, and settled down again to work, in the enjoyment of the *Sea Otter*. Of that steamer I can tell you little; for though she still pants her aged way among the inlets of the coast, my eyes have never chanced to see her. I could never get much more from Bill concerning her than that she was "a good little boat." But Jimmy Collins once told me a little more. "She was about thirty feet long," he said, "and her hull was fairly strong. The engines and boiler were middling good too; they were a bit too strong for the hull. Leastways Bill never dared give her a full head of steam, for fear of shaking her to pieces. It used to be a great sight to watch him in the engine-room. At the start he didn't know the first blamed thing about steam, and when the engines used to buck on him, him and Carter would spend hours crawling round with spanners and arguing about what was the matter. But after a while they got the combination all figured out, and they made the *Sea Otter* work good for them, towing logs to their boom and fetching freight from Alert Bay."

So Carter and Allen prospered in their hand-logging and soon had money in the bank. The next thing I knew of them was told me also by Jimmy Collins, and I think it is worth giving in his own words. "Just about then," said Jimmy, "old Cap Cohoon lost the *Midge*. Cap was a dandy. He'd had the *Midge* running two years after she had a piece blown out of her boiler. Cap just put a pad over the hole, and pressed a sheet of metal over that, and kept the lot braced tight against the side of the boat with a jack-screw. When the *Midge* got lost, Carter sold him the *Sea Otter* for five hundred dollars, and bought the *Ima Hogg*. That was just before Carter started business as a boss logger." Carter, in fact, had made enough money, by this time, to enable him to make a deal with one of the big sawmill companies. For so much cash down, and so much in half-yearly instalments, he bought a donkey-engine and its "rigging." Then he staked some timber leases, and set to work to put up buildings for a logging camp.

Now the country round about where Carter worked was becoming well known to logging men. A population of hand-loggers was stringing itself out along the shores; donkey-engine camps were starting up here and there; and the coasting steamers from Vancouver had extended their former course to take in the new business centre, Port Browning, where a store and a hotel had been established. So Carter went down to Port Browning and hired half a dozen men to work for him. Oh, the proud moment!

Now let me tell you that a logging camp is not an easy thing to run, successfully. A man may understand the practical side of logging — the ins and outs of the actual process by which the logs may be removed from a forest area and sent to market; or he may understand the business side of logging — the keeping of accounts, the knowledge of profit or loss, expenses, debts, assets, balance at the bank, and all that sort of thing. It very rarely happens that logging bosses understand both these sides, and the one they usually know nothing about is the business side. That is why so many of them

*"Then Carter bought the* Ima Hogg.*"*

come to grief, financially; for they engage in a business that is somewhat of a gamble, where money comes in quick and goes out quick in large sums, where a firm grip on business principles is very necessary, and often they are men with less power of grasping matters of simple finance and arithmetic than the reckless undergraduate, absorbed in "going the pace, blue." Carter's ideas of "figuring" were those of a child; he took wild risks in starting business as a boss; he knew he did. Yet a fine consciousness of his great power of blind, persistent effort made him careless of his own defects; and already, by some luck of judgment, he had schemed the policy that brought him to Success.

His capital was small, his means of doing work were limited. He had the sense not to attempt formal logging. He did not build logging roads and try to take, on any system, all the good timber that stood upon his leases, after the fashion of a high-class logging company. He worked, instead, close to the beach, cutting timber along the frontage of his leases, taking those logs only that he could haul out easily. One thousand feet, the length of his wire cable, was the farthest inland he ever went; and that not often. Much he cared that he was spoiling leases for future working, like a mine manager who should hurriedly exhaust the rich patches of his mine. Leases, he said, were going up in value. Someone would find it worthwhile, some day, to buy from him the stretches of forest whose sea-fronts he had shattered and left in tangled wreckage. As for him, he was going to butcher his woods as he pleased. It paid!

Now your logger likes to see artistic work done in the woods, and Carter's methods are distasteful to him. "Carter! gar-r-r! don't talk to me of Carter! *He's* no logger. *He* doesn't know how to log!" is a sentiment one often hears expressed. Carter hears of this, too. "I'm a Siwash logger,[1] am I? Well, I *am* a Siwash logger. Well, and what then? Answer me now!" I've heard him say, meeting the contempt behind the word unflinchingly, hiding his galled vanity . . .

So Carter from the very start set out to sack the woods, as

---

[1] Siwash logger = beachcomber of no account.

medieval towns were sacked, by Vandal methods. He staked or bought some thirteen leases, I believe, to provide himself with timber sufficient for such policy. He constructed his camp buildings upon rafts of huge great logs, purposely; he built another raft to take the donkey-engine; he held himself prepared to move at any time. For he meant to move from lease to lease, exhausting each of its sea-front timber; making quick money. And this moving forced him to great adventures.

# CHAPTER XII

# The Employer of Men

THERE IS NO single thing in his career that convinces me so much of the essential greatness of some parts of Carter's character as the fact that he has forced success to come to him as an employer of other men. For his task has been one of appalling difficulty.

The Western logger of the better sort is pretty free with his dislike, to an employer. A boss who hustles on the work, as Carter does, incurs a special danger of ill-will that can be averted, only, by special qualities of character—for hustling the work comes perilously near to hustling the men who do it, a thing you must not dare attempt with loggers. And yet a certain amount of hustle is essential.

To be efficient as a logging boss a man must not be too soft and easy-going, or else the work done for him will also bear that character and the logs he gets will cost him ruinously. Yet it is desirable that men should judge him as a "decent sort of fellow"; he must not be too hard, too grasping. He must not commit impertinence, advising or helping or criticising a man at work. Yet he must understand most thoroughly how everything should be done; and see that it be done the proper way; and give men the stimulus of knowing that they are working for a boss who can tell good work from bad.

Please allow me to escape from cataloguing all the stronger qualities of man; for I recall a scene on Thibert Creek that illustrates the fine, sensitive vanity of the best sort of Western working-men. The

mine boss, I remember, had come up the trail to where Bill Frazer
was working. "Enough work here to last you all summer, Frazer,"
he said genially, and passed on, pleased at the good work Frazer was
doing. Frazer pondered over the remark. At last he came to the
conclusion that what the boss had *meant to hint* was, "You are
working so slow, Frazer, that *it will take you all summer* to do this
trifling work." He dropped his tools and left the camp.

Imagine how unfitted Carter was to deal successfully with men
so sensitive. The dissatisfied look he wears upon his face would
ruffle their feelings, anger them, make them careless how they did
his work. Again, Carter has a fatal air of the confirmed schoolmaster.
He has been chastened by experience, and yet he has it badly even
now, for it is of the very essence of his character. He can never see a
man struggling with the difficulties of some job or other, he can
never see hurrying men checked by some necessary delay, without
throbbing with the desire to do the thing himself and "show them
ruddy loafers how to work." He has gained, through bitter episodes,
enough sense to restrain himself, often; but at all times he makes
men conscious of his contempt for their degree of skill, and of his
dissatisfaction at the amount of work they get through. He makes
them feel that they are just dead matter he uses for his own purposes, and throws away disgustedly when used. Men of any value
will not tolerate that sort of thing; especially as Carter's skill at any
given job does not inspire their respect. They work a week or so for
him, their dander rises, and they go.

So Carter in busy times can only keep his camp equipped for
work by aid of a continual stream of newly-hired men; and those
(because his reputation spreads abroad) are rarely of the better sort.
Think how difficult it must be, in a district far from places where
men can be hired, to secure this stream of men; think how difficult
to keep the stream steady, through steamboat accidents and foul
weather; think of the useless riff-raff that may be brought along with
it; and think of the enormous expense and the heart-breaking interruptions to the logging work. Good men, too, are more or less
essential for good, profitable working in the woods. Carter cannot

keep them! Never was man more handicapped by defects in his own character, less capable of moderating them. And he has had some sharp lessons!

Joe Collins told me that in the early days of his career as a boss logger Carter once quarrelled with a certain man in his employ. The man quit, and was about to use one of the camp rowboats to take his blankets and himself across to Port Browning. This was the usual practice in the camp. But Carter on this occasion hid away the metal rowlocks of the boats. He hoped to spite the man, to make him lose a week, perhaps, idly waiting for a boat to pass that way. He hoped to make the man pay heavily for his meals while waiting. And so he would have done had not his men all mutinied at the outrage. There were about twelve of them working in the camp at that time. Their simmering dislike of Carter's character boiled over. They quit suddenly, to a man. They threatened to tie Carter out in the sea until he should consent to find the rowlocks: they made him find them, made him pay all wages due. Then, taking all his rowboats, they rowed their cheerful way to Port Browning, and left the mortified Carter half crazed with futile hate. Nothing could have hurt him more cruelly. For to exert power over men is whisky to Carter's soul: it is the craving for crude power that drives him at his life's work. And here he had tried to satisfy his desire and had failed, and had been mocked bitterly.

Carter, however, is often successful in small tyrannies, especially in money matters. In these he is helped by the carelessness of those with whom he deals. For in the logging country nearly all business is done by word of mouth; contracts are made verbally, and registered only in the memories of those who make them; and when a dispute arises in the course of any settlement, it is no uncommon thing for each side to find itself unable to produce the least evidence in support of its own word.

Now I make no aspersion on Carter's honesty. I have heard many enemies of his declare that Carter intends, at any rate, to "give a man a square deal," and I myself have seen him do the fair thing with perfect naturalness when he might have done the other; and puzzled my brains in vain to find the reason why. But it is

obvious that the absence of business methods and written agree-
ments and formal understandings is to the advantage of a man who
has, like Carter, a blind confidence in his own memory, distrust of
the memories of other men, and a secret contempt for those with
whom he deals. In fact, were it not that his main energies are
devoted to toil and battle with the forest, Carter might find occasion
to make much profit from his dealings with lesser men: happy-go-
lucky loggers hired by Bill on some vague understanding about
wages; who have bought supplies from Carter without troubling to
ask about the prices; who have no guarantee of fair treatment than
that which their physical appearance and their power of injuring
Carter's reputation by talk in the saloons may happen to inspire in
Carter's mind. Such profit, however, won by such harsh confidence
in his own integrity, does not make an employer well spoken of.
Because of this Carter must secure the men he needs by temptation
of big wages, and even then he gets them ill-disposed. Without the
use he makes of Bill's popularity he could not hope to overcome this
desperate handicap to profitable work.

Bill it is who is sent out to hire men, and persuade storekeepers,
and humour creditors, and settle inconvenient lawsuits out of court.
Only once was Carter forced to leave his dear work and go to Vancouver to fight a lawsuit. On that occasion you might say that Carter
was victorious; for when the case was called the plaintiff was unable
to appear. He was found drunk, and the case went in Carter's favour
by default. But Carter paid most dearly for the victory: the visit to
Vancouver upset his fragile virtue, and the drunk he had to go upon
cost him two weeks of precious time and several hundred dollars
cash. So, should you ever wish to sue the firm of Carter & Allen for
wages due, take my advice and enter suit against Carter personally.
You will win your case; for he will be afraid to come to town. Carter,
then, bides close in his far camp, and sends Bill upon his errands.
And the two men are truly mated, as partners.

Carter, of course, can only tolerate a man who seems subser-
vient to his every whim; a man who will slave for him; who will
submit, in moments of Carter's anger, to be talked to like a dog. All
this Bill will do, and never turn a hair. I have heard men say they

have felt sick to hear Carter will often work himself into a fury over
Bill's shortcomings, and threaten to throw him out of the partnership, and say the most mortifying things about him — things that
men repeat to Bill, sooner or later. Hearing Carter's loud talk, you
would think Bill would often meet a stinging reception upon his
return. But no! A nasty gleaming look, a sullen remark or two . . .
and Carter's appearance will soften; and Bill will hear no more of the
threatened row. In fact, if Bill has taken care to bring up whisky with
him to the camp, Carter will soon be heard confiding to someone (in
the queerest voice!) that "Never had man such a partner. Bill's a
real fine boy; he's the straight goods! Don't let nobody never say
nothing to ME about BILL. D'YE HEAR!!" It sounds like repentance
prompted by affection. Carter and affection!

Bill on his side takes not the least notice of Carter's moods. He
does as he is told, biddable as a child. He shuts his ears to abuse; he
ignores contumely; he never makes the least complaint. And when
men ask him how he can remain associate, in partnership, with such
a man as Carter — and when they call Carter, as they often do, by
unpardonable names — Bill will flare up in loyal defence of the man
who uses him so badly. It is absurd to see so mild a man become so
quarrelsome.

"They name Carter a son-of-a-dog," he has often said to me
afterwards, bitterly, "and yet there's none of them men enough to
do what he has done, in work. And when he's drinking there are lots
of them mean enough to borrow his money, right and left, saying
bad things of him behind his back." Certainly Carter does give away
money when he is drunk. And I know Bill has had some painful
times when Carter has been drunk, pig-drunk, for seven or ten days
together, senseless and bestial upon Port Browning beach, the butt
and mock of hostile men.

Bill's admiration for his great partner glows visibly within him.
He would have played Boswell to Carter's Johnson. He yields to
hero-worship. And in this I feel Bill's sight is very clear. For among
the clinkers and the base alloys that make up much of Carter's soul
there is a piece of purest metal, of true human greatness, an inspiration and a happiness to see.

## CHAPTER XIII

# Hazarding the Donk

ONE OF THE GREAT moments in Carter's life was that in which he paid the last instalment owing to the sawmill and looked with proud eyes upon a donkey-engine that was his very own. There, close by the beach, lay the great machine, worth, with all its gear, five thousand dollars. There, Carter could tell himself, was the fine object he had won by courage and by sheer hard work. There was the thing his earnings had created. Past earnings were no idle profit. There they were, in that donkey, in material form, *working for him*—helping him to get out logs and rise higher to Success.

I make myself a picture, too, of an earlier moment in Carter's life—on the first morning when his donkey began its work. He sees smoke whirling up among the forest trees; he sees the donkey's smokestack above the rough shelter roof; the boiler, furnace, pistons underneath. And then the two great drums worked by the pistons, drums upon which are reeled the wire cables. And then the platform he himself has made, twenty feet by six in size, upon which boiler, engine, drums are firmly bolted: a platform that is a great sleigh resting upon huge wooden runners; hewn and framed together sound and solid.

Watch Carter when the "donk" (*his* donkey!) has got up steam — its first steam; and when the rigging men (*his* rigging men!) drag out the wire rope to make a great circle through the woods. And when the circle is complete from one drum, round by where the cut logs are lying, back to the other drum; and when the active rigging slinger (*his* rigging slinger!) has hooked a log on to a point of the wire cable; and when the signaller (*his* signaller!) has pulled the wire telegraph and made the donkey toot . . . just think of Carter's feelings as the engineer jams over levers, opens up the throttle, sets the thudding, whirring donkey winding up the cable, and drags the first log into sight; out from the forest down to the beach; bump, bump! Think what this mastery over huge, heavy logs means to a man who has been used to coax them to tiny movements by patience and a puny jack-screw . . . and judge if Happiness and Carter met on that great day . . .

*A donkey.*

Carter, you understand, does not belong to the class of *ingenious*-minded men. He is not skilful; he does not improvise ingenious makeshifts; he does not readily pick up new knowledge. When he bought his donkey, for example, he knew nothing about the care of machinery or the handling of engines, and he was a poor blacksmith and no mechanic. And he was slow to learn. So, for a time, he was obliged to depend upon hired engineers; to risk his precious donkey in the hands of men whose skill he had no means of estimating. But when he had gained a poor smattering of mechanical knowledge his rough self-confidence made him feel that smattering sufficient. Then Carter began to handle his donkey according to his own ideas.

Skilled artists—hook-tenders, rigging slingers, engineers—hated to work for a man who had never learned the ABC of classical methods. Carter did without such men. He went at every problem by the light of nature—"bald-headed," as the saying is—in furious attack. He would anchor out his wire cable around some tree, and make the donkey wind itself up mountain slopes, over rocks and stumps and windfall logs and all the obstacles of new-felled hillside forest. He would "jump the donk" aboard a raft from off the beach and tow it here and there along the coast. He did the things that skilled donkeymen can do. He handled his donkey in a stupid, clumsy fashion; muddling with it for want of skill, experience, and training; refusing assistance or advice from men who could have helped him. And yet he made that donkey go, in the end, where he willed it should go. He made it do his botching work, and made that botching work most profitable. He had no awe of his donkey, that great, awkward mechanism, nor of its ailments. He used it as in earlier days he may have used a wheelbarrow, as a thing that could be trundled anywhere, with freedom. But he had some heart-griping accidents. Once, I have heard, some stupidity of his allowed the donk to slide downhill and drop into the sea. Bill was despatched with the steamer to seek assistance, to ask some other logger to bring a donkey and, with it, drag the sunken machine to land. But no owner would expose his donkey to risk from wind and sea for Carter's sake. At last old Cap Cohoon came with all his men, bringing blocks and tackle and wire cables. His crowd and Carter's

men between them drew the donkey upright in the water. There it
stayed until the time of the "big run-outs," when the tides go very
low. Carter lit a fire in the furnace one night, got up steam, tied the
cable to a tree-stump near the shore, and made the donkey wind
itself up to the beach—just ahead of the rising tide. And so he
regained his donkey, his fortune. But the machinery was no better
for the adventure.

Another time when Carter was moving camp from Broughton
Island down to Gilchrist Bay disaster hovered over him for two
whole days. His steamboat, the *Ima Hogg,* was towing the whole
outfit down the channel; towing the raft on which the donkey stood,
the bunkhouse raft, the cookhouse raft, the office raft—a floating
village. Heavy blocks, tackle of all description, huge hooks, wire
cables, logging tools, boom chains, stores—every single thing that
Carter owned (except his timber leases) was on those rafts. Suddenly, in mid-channel, the *Ima Hogg* lost her propeller!

There were Carter and his hard-earned wealth left drifting at
random, at the mercy of the tides. Wind might be expected at any
moment in that neighborhood. Wind and sea would shatter his rafts
and buildings, after pounding them against the steep, jagged, rocky
shores... I have heard that Carter worked for forty-eight hours
fixing things aboard the rafts; and that having done his best, he went
to bed and slept. He and his men were found asleep by Bill, who
had gone with other men in a rowboat to search the channels for a
tug; who had after two days found one; and who had returned with it
in time to save the rafts and steamboat from their fates upon the
rocks. The weather had kept fine; the tides had merely swept the
rafts up and down in mid-channel; and Carter had had one of the
most marvellous escapes from ruin that I have ever heard of in the
logging country.

You might think that such an incident would have shaken Carter's nerve and made him shy of risking his donkey upon sea journeys. But barely six months later he hazarded his whole wealth
upon a venture bristling with risks, the great venture of his life that
brought him to the pinnacle of his success. It came about through
the agency of a man named Billy Hewlitt.

About this time, it should be said, logs were going up in price rapidly, and speculators had begun to realise that the forests suitable for logging (by existing methods) were limited in area and might soon be passing into private ownership. There arose, therefore, a great scramble to stake good timber leases. Parties of men explored the coasts everywhere for timber that was worth the staking; and other men in stores and barrooms and offices in Vancouver City gambled in leases of the timber that was staked. It was boom-time. Now Billy Hewlitt was a "timber-cruiser" — a man who sought for forest timber, to stake it; and Billy was hard up. For he was a man too hopeful, too enterprising. He had taken up timber leases in the most distant, unheard-of places. Dealers would not buy them — would not even send an expert to inspect them, so far away were they. The rent Billy had to pay the Government per square mile of lease was sucking his pockets dry. Things were thus going badly with him when, one day, he rowed his boat in to Gilchrist Bay and stayed at Carter's camp, storm-bound. Now Carter, working in his camp, had sniffed the smell of boom-time from afar. He had been cruelly torn in soul. He was making such good money, he was hurrying logs into the sea with such intense desire to profit by high prices, that he dared not leave his camp. Yet his gambling nature longed passionately to take a hand in the fascinating game of staking timber of which he heard such glowing accounts from recent winners. So when Billy Hewlitt spent an evening at the camp, and talked big about the wonderful good timber he had for sale, and backed his words with the logic of two bottles of whisky that he brought up from his boat, Carter's heart took fire. He ordered Bill to load the steamboat up with fir-bark and get her ready for a cruise next morning. Then he and Billy Hewlitt steamed away among the channels, on a tour of inspection of Billy Hewlitt's leases . . .

Carter bought all these leases; dirt cheap, of course, for Billy was no match for him in cold business duels. And thus it was that Carter came to own, among other claims, the two square miles of timber at the head of Coola Inlet. When the cruise was over and he was back at logging work his thoughts would often dwell upon those two square miles. For the sea-front timber there was very good.

There is talk enough of Coola Inlet elsewhere in this book, and after reading it you may have some respect for Carter's courage in the great enterprise he now undertook, after deep thought upon the recent purchase of Billy Hewlitt's leases. Remember that Carter, after all, was a "small man"—a man in a small way of business. His little capital was new-made; he might have made a cautious choice of safe investment for it; he might have kept on working as he was doing, under moderate risks. He might have known that he was forty-six years old, and getting older after a hard life. Instead of that, by one Napoleonic stroke, Carter decided to take a risk that would have daunted a young man with five times his capital, that would have made a rich speculative company think twice. He decided to shift his camp and donkey and to log the timber at the head of Coola Inlet, up among the feet of mountains, sixty miles of storm-swept water away from anywhere.

# CHAPTER XIV

# Carter in Apotheosis

W ITH CARTER ESTABLISHED in his camp at the head of Coola Inlet, Bill comes into prominence in the story. Bill himself liked working in the woods; he was a good axeman and loved chopping. But Carter made him stay aboard the steamboat, the *Ima Hogg*; keeping communication open between the camp and Port Browning. And Bill did that work with quiet faithfulness, journeying up and down the Inlet without much interruption for months at a time, and doing distasteful things in jeopardy of storm, discomfort, and indeed of wreck. A man I know told me about this steamboat work of Bill's, and I will repeat as much as I remember in the man's own word.

"The *Ima Hogg* was a godforsaken-looking tub. Her hull some way or other looked to be sort of lopsided. It used to give a fellow a sort of uneasy feeling just to look at it. On top she had a rickety old box of a pilot house with two bunks in it, and the engine room was all boarded in like an old busted chicken house, and patched with driftwood and strips off grocery boxes. Carter never cared how things looked so long as they did the work.

"Logging at the head of Coola Inlet kept Bill busy all the time bringing men and supplies up to the camp. Men wouldn't stay more than a week or two with Carter at the best of times; but when he'd shifted his camp up there, to hell-and-gone among them ruddy mountains, he simply couldn't get fellows to stay at all. I tell you I hand-logged one winter myself up round Kwalate Point, and I had all the Inlet I wanted before spring came. What with that gloomy scenery to look at all day, in winter, and what with lying awake at night listening to the roar of them rock slides and snow slides echoing back and forward from one mountain to another, it fair made me bughouse. Then the snow lies heavy in the woods up there, and men in Carter's camp could only work about fifteen days in the month in winter-time, and after paying for their board they made no money worth having, even if Carter *did* pay big wages. Of course in summer-time it ain't so bad up the Inlet. But work is plentiful everywhere then and men are scarce. So Carter was short-handed summer and winter. Holy suffering Mackinaw! don't you talk to me! Carter had the finest kind of nerve to start that camp of his up there!

"That Coola Inlet is a son-of-a-dog for *wind*. There's the west wind in summer, and the north wind and the sou'-easter in winter. They're all mean, and there's next to no anchorage. You get forty fathom right off the rocks most places. Then it's about sixty-five miles from Hanson Island, where you get into the Inlet up to the head, and next to no shelter. I tell you Bill had some fancy times with that steamboat of his. He used to run at night and get wood and water by day. He used to sleep when the weather would let him. Sometimes he'd get anchored and go to bed, and find himself ashore when he woke up. Other times the anchor would drag and he'd wake up in the middle of the Inlet. When he was running he would look at the fire and throw in bark, and get things straight in the engine room. Then he'd run forward to the pilot house and see where he was going, and take the wheel until he had to go and put in some more fire. It was a mean job for a man all by himself.

"I tell you the sea gets up terrible quick on that blank-blank Inlet. It is bad enough in a rowboat, but it was a damn sight worse on the *Ima Hogg*. You see, she had a fine upright boiler, but it was put in much too high. The least sea would make that old tub roll so's it would put the fear of God into you. Bill put in some fierce times jiggling her up and down all night behind some sheltering point of land when he'd been surprised by the wind and couldn't get to any anchorage. Sometimes it was lucky for him that he had passengers on board. One trip a gust of wind caught him unawares before he could skip to shelter, and it laid the *Ima Hogg* over on her side and the water came in through the rotten decks. There was a gang of fellows on board, going up to the camp. They jumped out of the pilot house (pretty slick, you bet!) and sat as far over as they could on the other side, and Bill got the steamboat turned so that the wind blew her upright again.

"Early this present summer Carter wanted Bill to run the donkey for him at the camp. So they put a young fellow named Cully on the *Ima Hogg*, and he ran her for a while. I don't pay no attention to talk myself. I know they used to fill the *Ima Hogg*'s tank with river water at the head of the Inlet, and my idea is that the water was brackish and that was what eat up the flues. Some says it was from being careless and firing up too quick that the flues got burnt out. There was a yarn, too, about someone putting blue vitriol into the boiler to spite Carter. All *I* know is that the last time Cully started up the Inlet one of the boiler flues was leaking. After a mile or two something blew out. Cully got it plugged and went on. As he was passing round Protection Point two or three more pieces blew out, and put the fire out. Cully just had enough way on to turn the *Ima Hogg* in to the bay beyond the Point and drift with the flood tide to where he could get anchorage. Before next morning he had everything plugged solid, and he put in a fire and got up steam. Then, pop! the whole works blew out ... Cully stopped in that place for two weeks, good and hungry, before Carter came down in a rowboat to see what the blank had happened. Carter saw that the *Ima Hogg* was out of business for a while, and he knew he couldn't afford to wait while she was being mended. He'd just *got* to have a steamboat taking men and grub up to the camp all the time. That's why he went on down to Hanson Island and bought the *Sonora* from Andy Horne for seventeen hundred dollars ..."

As you may imagine from this account, the quiet, unassuming Bill has useful qualities. You would be vividly convinced of that were you to see the steamboat that he ran and then see Coola Inlet. And should you wish to get new thrills from life, go you and buy the *Ima Hogg* yourself. She lies today mouldering at anchor at Port Browning, awaiting her next brave purchaser. Carter will ask six hundred dollars, but you might beat him down to three.

Now my story comes to the time last summer when Higgs and I

went timber-cruising up Coola Inlet. We had a fine west wind one day, and we ran our sloop before it up to the Inlet's head. There we coasted around the tide-flats that spread seawards from the river Kleen-a-Kleen, and suddenly we saw puffs of white steam upon a mountainside, and heard a donkey-engine toot. We anchored soon off Carter's camp, and went ashore to seek the usual hospitality.

It was a fine sunny day, and a man's eyes were pleased by the forest-green of the great mountains and the snowy whiteness of glaciers showing against the blue sky. The sea was sparkling in ripples against the gleaming line of Carter's boom, that lay across a little bay. In the still waters of that haven floated the rafts upon which the camp buildings stood—lake dwellings, as it were; and round them drifted logs; hundreds of logs, a carpet on the water; huge logs of fir and cedar. As we looked shoreward the air became filled with a rumbling, booming noise, and bumping down a hillside chute there shot into sight another log. It was fine to see the water shoot up in lofty jets and sunlit spray, as the log dived to join its fellows in the sea. Ten dollars more in Carter's pocket!

We tied our rowboat to the boom, and made our way over floating logs to a building from where stovepipe smoke was rising. Within we found the China cook, a spotless white-clad figure, engaged upon the work of dinner. John told us that "him bossy man" was working on the hill, and we went ashore to present ourselves to Carter.

After fires, or when some big building has collapsed, or when tornadoes have battered tropic forests into piles of fallen timber, men may have to work, walking and crawling, high in air among tangled beams and wreckage. In just such fashion men were working upon the mountainside near Carter's camp. As we slowly worked our way uphill we saw a sight that could not have been beaten in any logging camp along the coast. The "fallers" had worked along the slope, slope that was almost cliff; and all the trees of value had been felled criss-cross, upon each other and upon the mass of smaller trees their fall had shattered. The "buckers" had then wormed their way among that giant heap of trunks and limbs and matted boughs, and sawn the good timber into lengths. It was a fine piece of work, on ground so steep and rough.

We came to where the "swampers" were at work chopping limbs and brush, preparing the cut logs for hauling. Beyond them we could hear the shouting and the clank of metal blocks and the tap of a sledgehammer where the rigging-men were making fast a log to the wire rope with which a donkey-engine hauls. And then I became aware of Carter.

His coal-black hair stuck through the crown of a ragged old felt hat. His eyes, his beard, were black. Sweat dripped and glistened on his cheeks. A flannel shirt, all rents and tears, hung on his body. His dirty overalls had lost one leg below the knee; torn underwear was fluttering there. His spiked boots were good, as loggers' boots must be; so also were the stout leather gloves upon his hands.

Carter did not see me, and I watched him as he worked furiously. He stood upon a log some ten feet in the air. His active body showed in fine balance as he swung his double-bitted axe. His muscles sprang at each swift movement. He *whipped* his axe into the log he was cutting—*chop, chop, chop*—the hurried working against Time, not the leisurely chop that you may hear from a man felling timber. His breath was making the noise that hammermen affect—hiss, hiss, hiss—loud and sharp between each dig of the axe. I was wondering how many hours a man might hope to work at the pace Carter was going, when the booming of the dinner-gong sounded from the cookhouse down below. Carter, looking up, saw me for the first time, and we became acquainted . . .

Higgs and I stayed several days that summer at his camp.

It was boom-time then all up the coast, and speculation was ballooning higher than men had ever known before, and still no sign of bursting showed. Logs were up to ten dollars per thousand feet, board measure. Loggers and hand-loggers were doing desperate work, fighting against Time, to put in logs and sell completed booms while prices were so high. And so we saw great Carter, in apotheosis.

"One million feet I put in for me last boom," he said, with pomp, one evening as we sat talking in his office; "ten thousand dollars for the work I done in forty days!" And then he sneered angrily at the softness of hired men, and the monstrous wages he was paying to keep a crew at work upon his sidehill. "Now's the time I want good work done," he said, "while logs are high; and none of the men I get are worth a damn. 'Tis poor creatures they are; scared of a steep place; afraid of hard work and accidents."

But Carter had other business besides the logging done at his own camp. Men all down the Inlet were selling logs to him that he resold, in bulk, to sawmills at Vancouver. And the seashore round the head of Coola Inlet was dotted with the tents of hand-loggers; men outfitted, grub-staked, as one says, by him.

Carter, you understand, was living strenuous days; his mind scheming, his body toiling, to get logs quickly down his hillside to the sea. He had no time to give to other matters, and yet he gambled right and left in speculative ventures, on which he could not keep his eye. A sort of child's carnival of business reigned in his disordered office.

Men in rowboats were always coming to the camp to get supplies. "I'm too busy to attend to it now," Carter would say to them; "go and get what you want from the cookhouse, and ask the Chinaman to keep track of what you take." Piles of clothing and boots and tools and tobacco and other stores were lying littered on the office floor. "Take what you want," Carter would tell a purchaser, "and tell me some other time what you've taken. I've got to get back to my work now."

Bill was supposed, by Carter, to keep accounts; but he was rarely at the camp. He would come into the office before going to Port Browning on the steamer and tear a handful of blank cheques out of the book. As he needed them he would fill these up in pencil. Neither he nor Carter would know what cheques the other issued, nor take the least note of cheques drawn by himself. It was an anarchy. No Rake's Progress could have shown a worse confusion in money matters; and it was evident that, as in other logging camps, there was a definite limit of prosperity beyond which Carter & Allen's business could not go. Carter knew this too. "Me business is getting too big for me to attend to all by meself," he lamented to me. His success had been due, under luck, to his great blind force of perseverance, of strenuous personal activity. Simple work, done in his presence and by his aid, succeeded well. But now his business was calling for more complicated thought, for more organising power, and Carter, having not these to give, felt a loss of grip.

It was queer, then, to find Carter vain of his capacity as a businessman. Under rum he bared his soul to me one evening.

"I can make a deal with any man," he said. "Buying and selling is what I was built for. This here logging doesn't give me a chance; it ain't suited to me like what business is. *Buy* from them that has *got* to sell, and *sell* to them that is *obliged* to buy; and cinch 'em all good and hard—that's all the secret there is to business!" Carter, you might almost say uncharitably, oozed with desire to trade beneath three golden balls.

There was a certain narrow shrewdness, however, in Carter's careless methods. For these methods had the effect of encouraging carelessness in the men he dealt with. Hand-loggers around the Inlet, for example, would never know how much Carter was charging them for food and tools, nor how much he would, in the end, pay them for their logs. Sometimes they felt it would be rude to ask too many suspicious questions about small sums, small prices of their groceries; sometimes they did not give such matters thought. The future and its days of payment do not weigh heavily upon the logger's mind; he lives much in the present. He expects to meet hard treatment from "businessmen"—men of more active acquisitiveness than himself; men with whom he runs his bills. He does not, however, expect them to sack his pocket (as Carter sacked the woods) upon the first onset, upon the first account. So these loggers trusted all to luck, to Carter, and to vague verbal understandings, the exact shape of which, in Carter's mind, they did not clearly ascertain. They did not realise that Carter took short views in making money; that he did not care a rap for their future custom, or for a friendly name.

Carter in the end was bitter hard to all these men. For he made bad debts occasionally, in such long-drawn-out transactions, and burning to revenge himself upon the human race, he would fall savagely upon his debtors and their debts. Revenge it was. Carter in these money dealings had motives other than the itch for money.

Lust of power over men it was that hag-rode Carter in such matters, to his own hurt. He liked to feel his hands upon other men's affairs, diverting them, compelling them to suit his own will. Debtors were playthings for his egoism — egoism that had a fell malicious side.

The last evening that Higgs and I spent at his camp Carter was drunk upon some whisky that Bill had brought up on the steamer. Carter had been filling the office with his loud talk, and as we left to go aboard our sloop he came outside the door with us. He stood upon the raft, swaying unsteadily, and looked up at the moonlit mountain and waved his hand around.

"All *MINE*," he croaked — "*my* donkey, *my* camps, *my* timber, *my* steamboat there! *Fifteen* square miles of timber leases belong to me! *Money* in the bank, and *money* in every boom for sixty miles, and hand-loggers *working* for me, and ME the boss of that there bunkhouse-full of men! Tell them swine at Port Browning I done it all! I and the donk! *I !!*"

CHAPTER XV

# The Arrival of the New Gang

M Y IDEALISTIC SCHEMES and plans of life, like those of other people, are apt to be upset by the small motives — of pique, ill-temper, nervous distaste — with which my everyday decisions are often swayed. But as long as I can stand the disagreeable other qualities that he may possess, I like to be in contact with a *great man.* I like to work for a man who has real thoroughness.

Of course, the main reasons why I worked for Carter were my desire for some money and my pleasure in that mode of life. But, like other men, I should soon have left his camp in anger had I not had a feeling for Carter's superb quality. I liked to work for Carter. I liked his romantic battling with work, with nature, with the hostility of his fellow men. I liked his ascetic lack of compromise, and he and I worked many days together in that camp of his and did not quarrel.

One Sunday morning, as we came out from eating breakfast, we saw, with joyful eyes, a steamboat making for the usual anchorage — about a mile down-coast. It was the *Sonora,* Carter's steamboat, returning from Port Browning with the repaired machinery and a new gang of men. We watched a rowboat filled with men that left the steamboat and came unsteadily towards our camp. The boat reached the seaward side of our raft, and men began to disembark.

I saw how things were, and went across the logs to give some help. "Pleased 'make y' 'quaince, ol' boy," said the first man I hoisted by the arm; "avadrink!" and poked an uncorked bottle full at my face. Whisky spilled down my shirt. His hand was shaky. They were all drunk in that boat—all faint from drink—their movements sluggish and uncertain. But none were paralysed, and all contrived to walk, leaning upon my arm, into the haven of the bunkhouse. Pong Sam, the new Chinese cook, was sober. He fell to work at once and lit the cookhouse stove.

Carter was impatient to get the heavy pieces of machinery ashore and take them up the hill to where the donkey-engine stood, and get the mechanism into working order. But he saw at once that the new crew could do no work that day. He left me to saw the broken ends of logs, and took his rifle and went up on the hill to hunt for meat. So I sawed all day, and men, revived by little sleep, came staggering, from hour to hour, from the bunkhouse to offer me a drink and "get acquainted." The bottles were all empty by the afternoon. In the evening, as the whisky left them, men began to "feel bad." Then I returned their hospitality by serving out some bromide. That bunkhouse was a depressing sight.

On the morrow several men turned out from their uneasy beds when Pong Sam banged the gong for breakfast. But they were sick, their heads were sore, and when Carter led the way up the hill to work none of the new arrivals followed. All that morning Carter worked in a fury; but he realised how foolish it would be to try to make men go to work. New men are not expected to reach a camp sober . . . At dinner-time Carter and I and the old engineer that Bill Allen had hired to work as donkey-man were alone at table. The boys had already gone back to their beds after a sick pretence of eating.

"Guess I'll have to lay off this afternoon," quavered the old man; "my nerves don't feel good enough for work yet." It was an apology.

Carter was doing business on his plate, bolting his grub in savage haste. He looked up as the donkey-man spoke; suave and good-humoured, with a gleam in his black Irish eye that made me remember a purring panther at the zoo that once, in boyhood, I had tried to stroke through the bar. His voice was sweetly sympathetic.

"All right, boy—all right," he said affectionately. The old man was soothed.

Carter's hand came down swift upon the table and made the dishes jump. His voice crashed.

"But JOHNNY-ON-THE-SPOT in the mornin'," he rasped, "or, MIND, you take the steamboat down the Inlet. I'll have no blank-blank fooling in MY camp. WORK OR GET TO BLAZES OUTER HERE!" he bawled.

I wondered at the unnecessary brutality. The poor old cockney engine-oiler quivered like a frightened rabbit. But after dinner I went into the bunkhouse and found the old fellow relating his interview to the listening crowd.

"You don't want to worry, dad," said I, to comfort him; "that's only Carter's way of talking. He don't mean no harm." But the story had made its impression on the boys.

"Gee whiz!" said one, "this is Swift Camp. Hired and fired in five minutes!" And then understanding of Carter's guile dawned on me. He had simply made use of the donkey-man's meekness of spirit. He had dropped upon him hard, knowing that the old man would repeat the interview, and so contrived to tell the other boys that they were really required to work next morning. Carter knew that if he had spoken sternly direct to the hook-tender, that chieftain would have flared up, rolled his blankets — and quit!

That afternoon, as I worked near the camp, I had another taste of Carter's diplomacy. I heard him go to the bunkhouse and ask for the donkey-man.

"Come out," said he in pleasant voice; "I want to speak to you. You'll find me in the blacksmith shop."

A few minutes later I heard a peremptory voice saying: "Here! take a drink of this. Hi!! that's enough. Take that sledgehammer. Are you ready? Now strike! Hard! HARDER!!... Get your breath now. Whad'yer mean by coming to a man's camp drunk?... Strike! strike! Let her have it. Go on! strike!... Take another drink. That's the last you'll get. Now strike! GO TO IT!!... You oughter be ashamed of yourself coming here in that filthy state. Strike!... Sweat that blank-blank whisky out of you..." There was a sound of uncertain blows as the poor old fellow sweated himself back to health and work, helping Carter to forge some logging hooks.

I should have liked to have seen someone try to bulldoze my friend Fitzsimmons, who slept in the next bunk to me, in that manner. But it is a fact that the boys all went to work next morning.

Fitz was talking to me that evening as we lay, heads near together, in adjoining bunks. His voice was a quiet murmur.

"There's worse places than a logging camp," he said. "After a fellow's got over the first two days and can begin to eat, life looks good enough to him. Of course, them first two days is bad.

"I don't hold with all this taking of dopes. Some fellows are holy terrors the way they will mop up pain-killer when they're trying to brace up as the booze leaves them. Ginger, too, and scent, and cayenne pepper, and all them things. I've seen Siwashes get drunk on essence of ginger.

"Did you hear about that fellow last week at Charlie Hunt's camp? Charlie hired him at Hanson along with some other fellows, and brought them all to camp Sunday morning. The same night the fellow began to feel terrible bad. There wasn't no whisky in camp, nor no pain-killer, nor nothing. The fellow went and hunted in the cookhouse to see if he could steal some essence of vanilla from the Chinaman, and he found a strange-looking bottle. Smelt all right to him anyhow, and he drank her off, not knowing that the Chink had a sore arm and this was his carbolic liniment. Stiffened *him* out in good shape. Yes sir! Corpsed him good.

"No, sirree, when I have quit boozing I just take Nature's remedy. I go and lie on the beach and take a good drink of sea-water, and make myself good and sick, *and stand it*. It's healthier for a man that way, and he will be fit for work before fellows what uses dopes has got their nerves to stop shaking.

"I've no use for a camp where there's whisky brought in. 'Course a bottle once in a while don't do no harm. But lots of fellows are stopping in camp to keep away from the booze. Besides, when a man's working he wants to *work*. Work and booze don't mix.

"Ellerson's is the best built camp I know of: spring beds in the bunkhouse, and good buildings, and a white cook that knows his business. Fine pies he makes, and the finest kinds of cakes, and

*"There's worse places than a logging camp."*

there's always good syrup, and none of your cheap dried fruit, but good canned pie-fruit.

"In some of these small camps the grub's not much account. When a fellow's paying five dollars a week he expects to get white man's food. I know the bosses say that it costs them more than five a week to feed a man, taking into account the wages of the cook and flunky. But that's no reason for poor grub. I've been in camps where there was no eggs 'cept once in a while, and sometimes no fresh beef, and no syrup. I don't work for no blank-blank *cheap* outfits. I said that once to Billy Sayers when I quit him. Gee! but he was mad!

"Camp is all right if you get a good set of boys.

"Summer-time, of course, when there's work everywhere, a fellow can keep shifting every week or two until he finds a camp where the company suits him. But when winter is coming on, and so many camps is shut down, a fellow wants to get into any sort of camp he can and stay there; unless he likes to lie around the hotels dead-broke. Not that he'll make any money, not to amount to anything, in winter anyway. Laying off so much for the rain will only leave fifteen or sixteen days' work in the month — I've known it as low as twelve. Wages will be low too, and after paying for board a man will only be a few dollars a month ahead. It's kind of tiresome sometimes in winter; lying on your bunk reading magazines or them dime novels by the Duchess and Mary Corelli; or playing blackjack or seven-up; with the bunkhouse all steaming with clothes hung up to dry, and a steady drizzle-and-drip outside. Young fellows think they can work out in all weathers and never hurt themselves or get the rheumatiz. But I know better, and *I won't work out in the rain,* not for any blank-blank logging boss that walks."

Fitz's recent history showed me once more how little real chance the logger has to forget, and escape from, whisky. Fitz is a good fellow and not at all a "drinking man." But it happened that at the last camp where he had been working a hook, a sharp, heavy logging "dog" had lost grip of a moving log under the strain of hauling, and flicking round, had ripped a great wound down Fitz's leg. He had been carried down to camp, put in a rowboat, and taken to Port Browning, to the hotel. There he lay sleepless day after day in an upstairs bedroom, listening to the ceaseless din from the barroom underneath. Sympathetic men, more or less drunk, would pay him visits, and bring up glasses and bottles, and press him to drink with them in kindly fashion. So Fitz began to drink, and got drunk, and stayed drunk—his wound undressed and festering. Then Bill came round to hire men, and hired Fitz, knowing nothing of the wounded leg.

Fitz told me, as I washed and dressed his leg with antiseptic at the camp, "Things are looking awful queer down the coast, feller. I tell you I was glad to get this job from Bill, even to work with Carter. You mark my words—bad times are coming."

## CHAPTER XVI

# The Captain of the "Sonora"

I WAS JUST DROPPING off to sleep, for I had turned in early, when Bill Allen pushed open the bunkhouse door. He woke me up.

"Say, Mart!" he said, "there's a sackful of fittings for the donkey-engine been left down at Port Browning by mistake the last trip. Carter wants you to come along with me and fetch that up right away. I'll go aboard and get steam up. See if you can get a few loads of wood aboard."

I put on my boots, and lit a lantern, and went out on the raft to where, upon the seaward side, the steamer wood was piled. The night was very dark; rain soon soaked me to the skin. For the autumn rains had begun, and up in that northern logging country it rains steadily through the hours, night and day, day in day out, week after week. At least, that is the impression that a man gets when working in the open, though doubtless there are rainless mornings. But Vancouver in the south has a rainfall of seventy inches; and Point Grey, somewhere up north, has a fall two hundred inches greater; so the fall on Coola Inlet must reach a high figure, half-way, perhaps, between these numbers. In such a country you became so used to rain that you became almost forgetful of it. Dry clothes became a rare luxury. Your feet, of course, were always wet. To take your boots off and empty out the water became an unconscious habit...

You know the sort of thing you meet with on the prairies, on big farms where everyone is occupied with wheat or cattle, with large labours. There *is no time*, people say, to grow vegetables or to milk cows, or to do a thousand other minor things. Condensed milk is *good enough.*

In logging camps like Carter's you will find the same spirit. *There is no time* to mend this or paint that, or to put things away or keep them ship-shape. Some persons may think it poor policy to set men to work with damaged tools; but Carter had his own stubborn view of the matter. "I know the boats want caulking, and the houses want new roofs, and half the tools in the blacksmith shop are broke," he said. "I could put the whole gang on to fixing things for a solid month and still have a lot left undone. But I ain't going to. I find if things are just left alone men will do the work with them one way or another. They only spoil good tools and good things, and I don't believe they lose so much time, either, from not having things fixed good." That was why Carter's rowboats leaked like sieves, and why the bunkhouse was left in its half-collapsed condition, and why the *Sonora* looked dingy as a London slum, and why our clothes hung on us ragged. Every minor thing in Carter's neighbourhood had to give way to the essential—getting work done that would lead directly to *"getting out logs."*

So that night as I began to load wood for the *Sonora* I had to use a damaged rowboat, a boat that oozed water at every seam, and that leaked in little jets at every badly mended hole. In that sinking boat my journeys to the *Sonora,* a mile down-coast, were slow and laborious. I would row a few strokes with the work-eaten, defaced oars, gently—because the half-rotten rowlock cleats had drawn their nails and threatened to come loose; then I would bale furiously with a large bucket, standing boot-deep in the water; and so, rowing and baling, contrive to make my dark passage to the light that showed on board the *Sonora*. Then Bill would leave his engine-room repairs and help me throw my load of wood on to the steamer's deck.

The falling of the tide stopped these dismal journeys through the black deluge of the midnight rain. Bill and I went down into the engine room and there dozed, before the furnace doors, warm and steaming in our rain-soaked clothes . . . Dawn woke us. We got up steam and waited awhile for the thick rain-fog to lift from off the water's surface. When the shore and Carter's camp had come dimly into sight Bill and I heaved up the heavy anchor (after some panting), and Bill gave me a short lecture on the winding course that I must take among the shallows of the tide-flats. For he had decided to run the steamer up to camp, and to throw the remaining wood direct from the raft on to the *Sonora*. So he went back to his engines, and I entered the little bow-windowed room, the pilot house, in which stood the shaky steering wheel—and was a steamboat captain for the first time in my life.

I suppose I was a trifle worried—full of anxiety about my course; for I have but a confused memory of that next half-hour. The current of the ebb, I remember, kept sweeping me from the path I meant to take; and then the steamer's stern (that I could watch through a small window behind my head) kept swinging irresponsibly and forced me, nilly-willy, to go in mortifying curves. The turning of the wheel, the winding up of slack yards of steering chain, would seem to produce no effect upon the boat's direction. Then of a sudden she would yaw and point elsewhere; and I would spin a frantic wheel the other way—and so repeat my blunder. Behind all this immediate occupation of my faculties and strain of my attention there were nightmare thoughts busy at argument in some back region of my brain. I saw that I should have to come away from the camp stern foremost. How in the name of common sense did you steer a steamer backwards—how turn your wheel? It seemed obvious enough afterwards, and you may think that, with a mathematical degree, I should have understood the trifling matter at a glance. But I had never given the matter a thought until that sudden moment of confusion, and as I tried to convince myself of the obvious truth— the *Sonora* went bump upon the sands! The tide had failed us.

Now it appeared that the way the *Sonora* steamed backwards depended in a very slight degree upon the use I made of the steering gear; the rudder was too small, too little rigid, I supposed. So we bumped our way about those shallows, made desperate efforts to escape, pushed and strained our hardest with long poles—and by bare luck found our happy way again into deep water. I ceased to jangle signals on the engine-room bell. I wiped my face. My first attempt at steering a steamer had finished without actual disaster. Carter will some day notice, and wonder at, a fresh-looking dent in the *Sonora*'s bows. I did that on a corner of the raft.

So we fell again to loading wood with our old rowboat tender, and got our full supply. Wood was stacked beside the boiler, from floor to roof, in the engine room; wood was piled on deck all round the house—forward around the pilot house, aft around the towing posts. The *Sonora,* as one might say, bristled with cordwood. I jangled the bell and took the wheel, and off we went down the Inlet into the fog . . .

I had a chart of the Inlet beside me in the pilot house, and there was a compass swinging in a small box by the wheel. But the chart was in several pieces, frayed and effaced and coffee-stained; and the compass needle, as I soon found, had ceased to point towards the north. Also my ideas about the conduct of a steamer in a fog were second-hand—conventional.

So Bill left his noisy engines and came up to me after awhile.

"You don't need to go so slow," he said; "keep a hundred feet off the beach when you see it, and let her go full-tilt. Make your miserable soul happy. What does the fog matter? There ain't no rocks."

It was a new point of view for me—as far as steamboat steering went. But this same fresh lack of self-distrust, this simple-minded willingness to face every problem in life, every emergency, and to deal with it directly by the light of Nature, is a thing that one is always meeting in the West. Men trust their own judgment; their minds are not honeycombed with doubts of it.

We must have made wondrous zigzags from side to side of Coola Inlet. Dark mountain passes would loom up from time to time, at times to port, at times to starboard. Occasionally I would find myself steering end-on against some cliff. Or gaps would come now and then in the upper fog and give me direction—a glacier or one of the old discoverer's "high stupendous mountains" showing. But the hours passed and our progress down the Inlet was tedious and slow. So Bill asked me to steer round Kwalate Point and to run in to

Adams' place. There was no anchorage in that little bay, should either of the winter winds come up, but in the quiet weather we could tie the *Sonora* to a log that Adams had anchored out, and wait for the fog to thin.

This we did. We found the log and lay anchored to it, near the mouth of the creek that meets the sea just below Adams' house. Then we went ashore to get some steamer wood that Bill had once stacked there on the beach. As we made the last laborious trip in the leaky, half-swamped rowboat the fog began to darken at the approach of night. It was too foggy yet, we thought, for us to venture forth. We looked out on the incessant rain. Adams' camp showed cheerless, nearby in the mist. Adams and his partners, in two years' work, had taken all the easy-got timber near the shores. The men had gone away for good; their boom was gone, their house had been dismantled. And now without the friendly smoke and evening lamp-light of their tenancy, the house gave a last touch of desolation to the bare, ugly scene—to the litter of chips and rotten logs, broken benches and clothes, and rusty cans, to the stumps and fallen timbers of the clearing.

Bill called me to consider more serious things. There was no oil aboard for the lanterns, it appeared—for the lanterns in the engine room. As hunger took us we found there was no food aboard—nothing for us to eat except the small remnant of a dried-fruit pie and the shakings of a sack of flour. The pie we ate; the flour we made into a bannock and baked beneath the furnace bars. Bill boiled some tea—leaves and cold water set to boil together, to his taste. Then he turned in to sleep, and left me to keep a sort of watch. He thought the fog might lighten after midnight and let us journey on.

So by the poor light of a piece of candle I sat writing letters in that warm engine room. My clothes, of course, were soaked with rain and sea-water. The very paper on which I wrote was all crinkled with smudged drippings from my hair; the pencil marks ran smudges across each line of writing. The engine-room roof leaked strings of water to the floor; drops hissed into steam upon the boiler's surface. Outside with equal hiss the rain fell down into the sea. And every twenty minutes, in the pitch darkness, I clambered over tangled piles of wood on deck, and made a circuit of the ship. For the tide was ebbing strong; and you understand—the natural uneasiness of a steamboat captain on that the first day of his first appearance upon any stage.

I remember that I was wishing that I had had some oilskins; though they are uncomfortable and hamper a man at any work. Just about that moment the accident occurred.

## CHAPTER XVII

# The Grounding of the "Sonora"

THERE WAS NOTHING to see in the darkness, and nothing to hear but the sizzling of the rain upon the sea and the rustling of the tide. The ebb was running, but for some reason our stern pointed to the shore.

To be anchored in that unknown place in a big ebb tide—a "long run out"—made me uneasy. I took a long pole from off the deck-house roof and prodded into the dark water at the bows. I could not touch the bottom. So then I fumbled my way aft, over the stacked wood, and tried the water with my pole. Heavens! it came as a shock to find there were but seven feet of water under our stern. We had taken ground that morning at the camp, but I had no clear idea of how many feet of water the steamboat drew. "How many feet? Were we aground?" I asked myself in horror.

I put my head in at the cabin door and spoke to Bill. I spoke in a tone of cautious anxiety, concealing alarm. I did not shout or show excitement, because I was afraid of making a fool of myself about nothing.

Bill said, "Oh, give her a prod out with a pole," and, bored with the incident, turned over in his bunk and slept again. I clambered, rather feverishly, amidships, where I could get good purchase for my poling; and finding bottom for my pole, began to push and squirm and push. The push soon told; the *Sonora* began to move, and my heart beat again. Then the fog lifted slightly for a moment, and, oh horror! I saw that the *Sonora* was only swinging round. Her stern was stuck!

My yelp brought Bill out of the cabin in one jump. He tumbled about in the darkness and found a pole. Both of us rushed aft and got a purchase on the ground and gritted our teeth and pushed desperately. Sweat broke out (as the saying is) on our foreheads when we felt it was no use. Realise if you can Bill's feelings. There was his steamboat—fond and proud of her he was in his secret heart. She represented hard-earned savings; she represented Success. Her money value was part of the little "stake" he had created and preserved amid the disasters of logging life—the little stake that one day, he hoped, would enable him to stop gambling with Nature on these inlets and buy him peace and safety on a little farm. There was Carter, too, to think of; and Carter bereft of his steamboat was an ominous figure to think of. Carter dearly loved to gall men who disliked him by taunting them with his own success. His ownership of the *Sonora* made a favourite taunt.

And now the *Sonora* was in great jeopardy. The Inlet everywhere is very deep. It is but a giant canal, like a canyon among the mountains, and filled with sea-water to depths that the Admiralty chart ignores. "So many fathoms and no bottom" is the usual sounding given, even near the shores.

But where creeks and rivers meet the sea small flats have been built out, continuing, under water, the flatlands of the little wooded deltas at the river mouths. The seaward edges of these flats break off in steep sudden slopes that drop precipitous to the Inlet's bottom at the angle that you see in high embankments on the railways. "The drop-off" men call these slopes. In such places a boat coming in to anchor will at one moment get no bottom for her sounding line; at the next moment get a moderate depth; at the next will float, in somewhat shallow water, over the river flat. In our case, you understand, the *Sonora* had stuck by the stern upon the sand. Forward there was deep water. Thus the steamboat lay across the drop-off's very edge—half of her keel upon the flat, half projecting out over deep water . . .

The tide was falling. Would the boat lurch over, forward and sideways, and fill and sink? The furnace was glowing hot beneath the boiler. What would happen in the engine room if the cold sea should pour in? Would there be explosions?

Realise if you please my own feelings. Here on my first command, on the first day of my captaincy, I had got my boat aground. She might tip over and be gone at any moment. Bill's boat: remorseful thought. Carter's boat. I should lose my job. My opinion of myself hurt me. Then there was the mortifying picture of the future; my dear self as a conversational figure, "the man what lost Carter's boat"; and the brand of incompetency. We had no tide tables — when would the tide cease falling? "Gee-sus-gee-sus-gee-sus," moaned Bill suddenly. He *had voiced his despair first*: it was (naturally enough) greater than mine.

Immediately my opinion of myself rose like a lark. I had not given myself away. I felt so superior to the man who had entertained despair; I felt I could show him how to keep cool and competent. The patronising "Don't get excited" came to my lips; it was with difficulty that I spared him that. I liked myself immensely in my new role... It certainly was a beastly job. We had to be swift, swifter, swift. There were things that had to be done at all costs, right away.

Bill dived into the engine room, and burning faggots of wood came circling out and fell hissing into the sea. He was drawing the fires, that furnace and boiler might have a chance to cool before the catastrophe. By the expiring lights of these floating faggots I could see to draw the rowboat alongside and to bale her with a bucket; with swift spasms of movement we piled into her, with an axe and the butt-end of a candle, rowed furiously through the darkness to the shore below Adams' house. The rain sizzled steadily on the sea.

There are always odds and ends of wood lying in the slashed timber that lies around a house; we wanted post lengths eight or nine feet long and about the thickness you note in light scaffolding. Imagine if it was an easy job to find them! We tripped and flopped and clambered over logs, and ran into things, and felt with our hands in the darkness. Somehow we found poles that would do, and one man held them while the other chopped them to right lengths with the axe — in darkness.

Then there was the rush back to the *Sonora,* now tilted over somewhat to starboard. That tilt served our purpose; we could jam posts under her on that side and she would rest upon them solid. We could make her safe sideways. As for the danger of her tipping forward, there was no use worrying about that — nothing could be done to avert it.

Perhaps you think it sounds easy to jam posts under a steamer. It is not. Imagine yourself alongside in a rowboat. You poke a post straight down into the water. The post does not want to go; it wants to *float* horizontally. There is a struggle before you get the foot of the post solid against the bottom. Then you press the post against the sloping side of the steamer and try to hammer it tight with the flat of an axe. The foot of the post gets clear of the bottom and up it floats; or your boat moves away with the recoil of your blows — and you lose grip of the post and lose your own balance, and the post is lost in the darkness. Later on you get in several posts, good and solid, and the next one you hammer in too tight, and the others, relieved of the strain, fall out and float away... Oh, it is pleasant work... And we were doing this sort of thing while a drumming in our ears said, "Quick, quick, quick," and the tide kept dropping, and the *Sonora* leaned more and more solidly over to starboard, and the world was all rain and water and darkness.

The posting was finished at last; we had done our best. We sat in the warmth of the engine room waiting for events. When would the tide stop falling? Would the *Sonora* keep from tipping down the "drop-off" till then? We sat in the darkness waiting, with a tummy-ache feeling inside us, deadly depressed. There was nothing to eat and we were tired.

The tide did not fall as low as we had feared; the steamer remained settled upon her posts, and in the early hours of the morning we too, like men reprieved, rebuilt the fire in the furnace and felt the *Sonora* begin to float again. We got up steam and put out again into the foggy Inlet, continuing our voyage to Port Browning. Dawn saw us passing Boulder Point; engines labouring at full pressure; Bill trying to make up for precious hours lost.

From the barroom of Port Browning Hotel Bill and I floated wearily into the restaurant—and began to eat. Two days—and we had had almost no food; two nights—and we had had almost no sleep; long-drawn hours of vanity-racking anxiety, working nearly all the time and soaked with rain—I tell you we wanted food that night. We ate good.

Then, if you must know, we had some whisky; and sat awhile in the comfortable warmth and unearthly brilliancy of the barroom; and then somehow a magic boat wafted us, like the body of King Arthur, over the black water, through the dark night. Goodness knows when or how or why the *Sonora* crossed our path. I can only tell you that Bill and I woke up on board, next morning, lying in our bunks—boots on and clothes sopping wet. We were hungry still, and we went ashore and had a good breakfast at the hotel.

After that we found the sack of castings that Carter had sent us to fetch. We loaded also on to the *Sonora* stores for the camp—cases of eggs, canned milk, canned cream, canned peas; fresh meat and sacks of cabbage and potatoes; butter and kerosene; smoking and chewing tobacco; working gloves, socks, and rifle ammunition. These we piled upon the deck forward, against the pilot house. Aft we had a weighty load of boom-chains and supplies for the black-smith's shop . . . Time was our ceaseless enemy, on the *Sonora*. Yet Bill must needs go ashore to the store, to the hotel, lounging about in conversations. You in your ignorance might have thought him loafing or engaged in social pleasure; but the fact was that he was attending, most severely, to his business. He was doing what the manufacturer does when he pores over the "City Column" and "Market Movements" in the trade journals. He was gleaning ideas. The casual talk of logging men was his newspaper.

A man in this country does not walk right into a store or a hotel and ask point-blank questions about what he wants to know. *I* do that sort of thing sometimes, and very disconcerted I become. That

*The Sonora after an accident.*

is because I am impatient and want to find out things at once; forgetting that very little can be torn out of a man by a direct question. There is no means of gauging the value of isolated statements made in hasty answer after the mental shock your question gives. You must let conversation *grow*, not tear it up to see the roots. You see, the logger is not an introspective person. He does not take the faintest interest in his own psychology. Unless he has some very definite reason, he does not at any given moment take the remotest interest in yours. He has not the habit of making rapid wrong pictures of your state of mind and of putting himself in your place; a habit that makes civilised intercourse so much quicker and easier. Besides, if you are a logger yourself, a man occupied in struggles with Nature and natural objects, you do not cultivate the power of cross-examination.

Therefore, to get the latest news about the demand for logs, the trend of prices, or the rate of wages, or the supply of men, Bill just drifts into the hotel or the store, and sits on a box within spitting range of the stove, and chews. Talk will be going on; all sorts of news that has an important bearing on his business will come out, in casual, desultory fashion, from time to time. Bill may guide the conversation a little; he hears what is said; he can watch the men who argue. Afterwards you find that he has gained impressions and drawn conclusions, and you wonder at the shrewdness that can divine so much from so few spoken words.

During these labours at Port Browning, and afterwards on our return trip to the camp, both Bill and I had a crushed feeling in our self-esteem. We had talked to one another about that accident, and proved to each other that we could not be held to blame for what had occurred, and yet we felt exactly as if we had blundered from incompetence.

## CHAPTER XVIII

# The Spirit of the Thing

THAT CARTER AND ALLEN outfit pleased my soul. All my days I have been looking for the strenuous, hoping to find and to work for men who should be really intense in their efforts to do things. Giblin used to say in his argument-annihilating way that the people I dreamed of did not exist. But they do. I found several of them in the northern logging country. There was Carter, now; Carter working his uttermost, plugging sternly at his work, day in day out; developing the energy of two active men. Yet his heroic soul would burst with impatience that he could do no more. I amused myself one day composing Carter's prayer, or rather exhortation to the powers. I will suppress the text. But it was all about the distressing shortness of daylight, the interruption caused to work (even to Carter's work) by darkness, the waste of time at meals and sleep, and the appalling listlessness of hired men. The exhortation ended with Carter's war-cry: *"Go to it, then! Do something!!"*

I know now that my judgment of a certain Pharaoh was too hasty. The man who wanted bricks made without straw was a great man — a great hustler. He was of kin to Carter. He wanted *efficiency*; he wanted men not to depend on others, helplessly. He wanted to instil his own great spirit into them, so that they would say of their own accord: "We possess no means of doing this job; never mind, we can do it all the same." And he would make the money...

There was Bill Allen, too, with his — "I tell you a man has got to hustle to make money logging." His motto for the steamboat was,

"Get wood and water by day; run by night; keep-agoing-all-the-time"; a sort of sing-song. You would have failed to give him credit for such spirit had you judged him by appearances, for he was not rude and volcanic, and obviously a man of action, as Carter was. Bill's manner was subdued and absentminded, his movements quiet. Nothing about him kindled your imagination. He seemed effaced in character. His face was pretty, framed in fair curly hair. When clean it had a weather-beaten air that had been girlish once; when smudged and engine-dirty it made you think, in ignorance, of a work-weary Willie. In those rare hours when nothing needed his attention you might see Bill poring over book or magazine, lost to the world, his every sense absorbed. The humour of a Sunday paper, Ouida, "The Duchess," "The Master Christian," *Science Jottings,* the *Nineteenth Century* would carry Bill, all equally, into some weird fairyland. "The Wrecker" held him spellbound too. Never, you would feel inclined to say, watching him, lived a man less practical, less of a worker. And Carter used to burn his books on the quiet. But Bill would "keep-agoing-all-the-time." In a gentle, persistent way he would work straight on, day and night, when needful; steadily on until sleep would drop him. He had a dreamy sort of way of dealing with difficulties and hindrances and pushing them aside without thinking. His subconscious mind was always wrapped in the idea of "getting the job done."

I liked the spirit of the thing; the quiet feeling that it is natural and right that a man should never admit that he cannot do a thing; the feeling that things *must* be done, done "right now," kept on at until they are done; that you have "got to get a move on" and work quickly. Not *if* the weather suits, or *if* circumstances are favourable, or *if* your calculations were correct, or *unless* you should be too tired . . . There was very little *if* or *unless* about Carter and Allen. Bill had had a man working on the *Sonora* the previous summer. Sometimes when dark was coming on the steamboat would be short of wood and near one anchorage and far from the next. The man would say, "Hi, Bill! what do you say if we anchor here? After a proper night's sleep and in daylight we'll be half the time getting wood, and we'll be just as far ahead at the end of twenty-four hours. We'll have to sleep some time." I can imagine how Allen would poke his head out of the engine-room door and look at the shore and sky, and pretend, politely, to consider the man's proposal, and then say in his mild voice, "I don't think it, Bud. Guess we'd better keep agoing. It might come on a headwind or something might happen. We'll go ashore with the lantern and chop wood, and then hit right through and sleep afterwards." That is Bill's style. He does not put off work. So I liked working for Carter, and working hard. As for Carter, he sized up the part of my work that he saw for what it was worth to him, disbelieved in the rest; apparently found that he was not losing on my wages (or he would have fired me), and did not give a cent how I felt about it.

I was steering through the long night, one trip, and old Andy sat with me in the pilot house. We were taking him up to Carter's camp, near which, the previous summer, he had found and staked a vein of mineral. Two "monied men" from Vancouver slept in our cabin aft. Andy was hoping that they would buy his claim. He was an old prospector.

We whiled away the hours in that pilot house by conversation. I talked of "the West," and of its spirit.

"Young man," said old Andy, "*don't you never say you don't know how to do a thing.* Let the boss find that out and do the worrying. You go ahead every time and tackle the job by your own sense. Nobody's going to have confidence in you unless you show them you have confidence in yourself. *That,* sir, is the *Western Spirit* — the spirit that has made the West what it is.

"It's queer to me," he went on, "the poor-spirited way Easterners and city folks and Englishmen go about their work. Seems as if the effect of education was to take all the enterprise and natural savvy out of a man. They come across some job they haven't done before, and they'll think of course they can't do it, and they'll sort of wait for someone to show them how to do it; or else they'll expect someone to send for a first-class man who's been at that job all his life. They're always distrusting their own judgment, and willing to believe that everyone else knows better and can give them advice worth following. They've got no natural get-up to them.

"I remember when I was a young fellow — just a boy you might say — I was working down in Oregon, 'swamping' in a camp there. I was a stranger in those parts, and I'd only been a day or two in the camp; and it was my first job in the woods. The foreman came to me. 'Tomorrow,' he sez, 'I'll take you off swamping and give you a job barking up at the head of the new skid-road.' I guess he thought I'd be pleased. Well, I had sense enough not to say nothing. But I went up that road after breakfast next morning expecting I'd be sent down to get my money soon as anyone seen me at work. I'd never barked a tree in my life. However, the boss didn't come round where I was working that day. There was another fellow barking where I was. I watched him out of the corner of my eye to see how he worked, and I just piled in and made the chips fly. I seen the other fellow take a queer look at me once in a while when he thought I wouldn't notice, but he kept on working and never said nothing.

"Same next day. I was working like blank (being but a boy with no opinion of myself) to make a good showing before the boss should come round.

"The third day the other fellow got talking to me. 'Say, kid,' he sez, 'you seem a pretty hard-working sort-of-a-feller. I guess you ain't never done no barking before — eh?'

" 'That's so,' sez I.

" 'Well,' he sez. 'I'll tell you. *You're taking the bark off the wrong side.*'

"Then he showed me how to take off the bark just along the side where the log would drag along the ground when being hauled. He useter mark the logs for me on the 'ride' and then I'd bark them. After a while I got to have some judgment as to which way up a log would ride, and then of course I was all right."

Old Andy, once started in this vein, went yarning on.

"It's always the same way," he continued. "I don't say but what a fellow wants to exercise judgment. But when in the course of my life I have undertaken a new job that I knew but very little about, my experience always told me that I was going to handle that job as well as the next man — *good enough*; unless the boss should fire me, or unless there should be some accident before I had had a chance to discover what were the difficulties I was up against.

"No, *sir*! There's nothing *to it* but having a hopeful mind and judgment and observation. How d'you think any work would ever get done up in these uncivilised parts unless there were men here that had hopeful ideas?

"Look at the mining business; old fellows working away in tunnels all their lives (the storekeepers getting what they make), and hating to die at the finish because they know there is rich pay a few feet beyond the face. Did you ever meet an old placer miner but what knew of one or two little places where a man might put down a shaft or run a tunnel and strike a big thing?

"How are these here prospectors for hopeful ideas? Getting out into the woods every time they've got a few dollars or got some mug to grub-stake them; cracking rocks on river bars; crawling round on mountains all by their lonesome; nosing about in the desolate, howling, ruddy wilderness by the month and by the year; and having a fit every time they see a ledge that looks like it might contain mineral. Of course, most of them take life pretty easy and aren't in no hurry at their work, and you might think they was loafers. But they're a hopeful class of men. Just you see the rubbish they pack into the assay offices . . ."

I used to be glad to get a stray passenger on board who, like old Andy, would help me to keep awake by talking. For often in that pilot house the night would pass with painful slowness. Perhaps Bill and I had been up two nights running, and I would be feeling again the tortures of sentry duty, the struggle against sleep. Sometimes I would not dare to put my *hands* upon the spokes of the wheel, for fear of standing asleep. I would steer with my *fingertips*; and then as sleep would make me lose my balance my head would hit the window frame and wake me up. Then I would hear the strokes of the engine becoming slower, feebler, and know that steam was going down — that Bill had been struck into sudden sleep while at his work in the warm engine room.

After such nights as this the cold light of dawn would perhaps be showing through the drizzle as we would creep up to the usual anchorage, our trip completed. Weary and sluggard the two of us would dump the anchor overboard, draw the fire in the engine room, load our freight into the rowboat, and start up coast to

Carter's camp. Breakfast in the camp cookhouse, we would feel, would be better than the trouble of cooking on the *Sonora* and eating the meal of syrup and corn-meal porridge which was our usual compromise with Time. The warm bunkhouse would be a fine place to sleep in afterwards — for we would be feeling chilly and wet and washed-out for want of sleep.

We would reach the camp and open the cookhouse door, and feel how good it was to take our seats alongside the boys at breakfast. The lamps would be lighted, for it would be still dark indoors at half-past six; the cookhouse would look bright and cosy — stove-wood stacked all round the walls, breast-high; slabs of bacon hanging from the roof above; canned stuff — peas, beans, tomatoes, fruit, syrup, beef, mutton — bright and shining, neatly piled on shelves; sacks of onions, potatoes, rice, beans, flour, at the far end where Pong Sam in spotless white would be busy at his stove — flapping hotcakes with swift, sure movements, bringing plates piled with them to table, answering calls for tea and coffee. Someone probably would have been out a few days before and shot a buck. The fried meat would smell good and look good upon the long table among the plates of fried ham, beans and bacon, potatoes, butter, syrup, cream and milk, and good yeast bread . . .

Carter would be sitting among the crowd at breakfast. He would scowl at us as we would enter.

"I thought you was never coming back," he would say in rat-trap tones; "whad'yer bin doin' all this time?"

Men to Carter are distastefully imperfect means that have to be used, unfortunately, in getting work done. They are just tools.

Whenever Carter thinks of them as human beings his manner becomes sour, hostile, ungrateful.

# CHAPTER XIX

# Steamboating on the Inlet

T HE SONORA HAD ONCE steamed from camp to Port Browning in twelve hours — seventy-five miles. So we always thought
of the journey to that port as a twelve-hour journey. It became a
habit to do so, especially with Carter. And every trip Bill and I
would howl to the men working on shore as we would row past on
our way to the anchored *Sonora,* "Bet you we make the round trip
in forty-eight hours this time!"

It came to me as a shock the other day to realise that our trips
took five or six or seven days. There was one record trip, done
under four.

The queer thing was that we never lost the hope of making a
quick trip — next time. *This* time our record was plainly spoiled:
there had been errors of judgment; we had lost hours and even days
by want of forethought, by carelessness that seemed gross when
looked back upon, by accidents out of the common. Carter would
have reason for sarcasm this trip. We used to pant to get it over, that
we might make another trip in the really competent manner that we
knew to be natural to us. We felt like the hundred-yards sprinter
who has stumbled in his start.

Perhaps our chief cause of delay, on the *Sonora,* was the battered old rowboat we towed astern. Whenever the wind would raise
the short, choppy sea of the Inlet that boat would become a nightmare worry; captain and engineer would fret uneasily at their work;
every few minutes one of them would grope his way over the wood

piled on deck and peer out into the darkness astern, and try the feel
of the tow-rope, and judge by the sound of thuds and splashes how
much water was in the boat behind. Every now and then one man
would call for the other's help, and the two men would haul the boat
close enough for one to jump in and bale with a bucket. A cold, wet
job, standing shin-deep in water, clothes soaked with the spray,
hands chilled by the wind; man and bucket going splashing asprawl
at every random jerk of the tow-line.

There were times, too, when we would forget the rowboat,
times when our thoughts were busy over some infirmity of the
engines. Then the leaking rowboat would get low in the water, a
wave would swamp her, another wave would throw her water-laden
mass with sudden jerk on the tow-line; and the next time one of us
would come to see, there would be no boat astern, but only an end
of torn rope. So we would turn the *Sonora* and roll and toss, circling
and zigzagging over the dark water, searching for a darker patch that
should prove to be the lost boat. No matter now if we should waste
an hour or two and use up good fuel. As long as any hope should
remain we must wander and seek; for without a tender we should
soon be crippled—without it no fuel could be got aboard.

It seems strange, now, that so forlorn a quest should have been
so often successful. We lost, as a matter of fact, but three boats all
winter; we must have searched, in hard squalls, in darkness, perhaps some twenty times.

Why not have hoisted the rowboat to its proper place, on the
deck-house roof, you may ask? Well, that brilliant idea occurred to
Bill and me one stormy night, and we fixed an ingenious system of
blocks and tackle to the windlass and gained an enormous power
over the soggy weight of the rowboat. The windlass turned, the rope
kept coming nicely; only when one of us went to look did we find
that the boat had not hoisted. The high arches of the iron davits had
bent down instead, and the *Sonora,* on the starboard side, had
gained (for ever, I suppose) a more wreckish air.

Carter used to boast that his steamboat need never stop on
account of wind and sea: a truthful boast. I have known her speed
drop to one mile an hour, or even less, against north winds in the

Inlet; but she could be depended on, absolutely, for that unless something unusual was the matter with the machinery. If we could have carried enough fuel to maintain these lesser speeds over sufficient distance, and if we had had no rowboat dragging behind and liable to sudden loss, bad weather would never have stopped us. For it did stop us — often. Perhaps you realise how these stops were forced upon us. It was true enough that wood and bark for sixteen hours' steaming could be carried on board — we would often start from camp with that full load. But once on our way we depended upon small replenishments of our fuel supply. For instance, down at Boulder Point, where the three Frenchmen had been hand-logging, there was a good deal of bark in the woods very close to the beach — the slope was very slight there, and the Frenchmen had had to bark their logs in coaxing them to water. These great, sturdy slabs of fir bark were excellent slow-burning fuel. We would heave them from one man to the other, and then down on to the beach and into the rowboat, and one baling, one rowing, would ferry the disorderly load aboard the *Sonora,* and start off again upon our interrupted journey. There were few such beaches in the Inlet. In most places the mountain slopes plunge straight into the sea. But here and there we knew of little spots where driftwood might be found, and where two hours' axework would give us a boatload or two of chunks and limbs and bits of bark. We would take anything that could be made to burn. Bill, besides, knew of a few places where hand-loggers had barked big fir logs up on the sidehill near the water; and sometimes, by careful watching of the passing forest, we would divine new places. Then one of us would go ashore and climb up the rocks, and pitch slabs of thick bark down into the sea, and so obtain the best of fuel.

But storms and headwinds spring up on short notice in the Inlet, and how could one man get fuel and load it from the beach into a leaking boat half-aground, and yet save the boat from bumping its bottom out amid the breakers, while the other man was obliged to remain busy as captain and engineer on the *Sonora,* cruising off-shore? And how, without more wood, with perchance but five or six hours' fuel on board, could a miserable old derelict like the *Sonora* be expected to bash her way through a head sea to an anchorage that might be thirty miles away? Such problems were not always easy for us to solve in that cold, wet, windy weather — nor pleasant.

There were times, however, when we had passengers on board, and passengers were welcome. For Bill and I were always sleepy on our trips, as we would try to run both day and night. Passengers could stoke and steer and let us get some hasty sleep. Our only trouble was their carelessness.

We left Port Browning, for example, one evening about dark, towing a rowboat for two hand-loggers who were returning to their camp. The men were on board. One volunteered to work in the engine room; the other, Jimmy Hill, went to the pilot house and steered. Bill and I escaped to the cookhouse to cook an evening meal. We were hungry, and we knew that we should be up all night.

The night outside was pitch black. The faintest kind of sheen showed on the water just around the boat; by staring hard, straining your eyes and twisting them and looking sideways, you could just see the change of hue, the variation in the blackness, where shore came down to water. That was what the steersman could see from the dark pilot house. Looking from the door of the lighted cook-house we could see black nothing. You understand, of course, that on the *Sonora* we never carried lights except in the cookhouse and the engine room.

Jimmy Hill knew those waters well, so Bill and I cooked at our ease. The engine, we could hear, was working in quick time, and a swift tide was running with us. We were going fast. We expected to hear Jimmy slow down soon and turn into that winding, narrow piece of water between Low Island and the southern shore of Western Channel. Steering down that piece of water used to make me sweat gently even in the daytime. In the dark it was far worse — a perfect nightmare of a place. I was glad so good a man as Jimmy was at the wheel ... There came a sudden shock that threw me up against the cookhouse wall and sent our pans and dishes flying. Then bump, and scrunch, and bump again. The *Sonora* shuddered from end to end and became still.

Bill dashed from the cookhouse and ran forward. I followed with the lantern, to find Bill and Jimmy leaning from the bows. Below, framed in the flat blackness, jetty shining surfaces reflected the lantern light. They were the boulders of Low Island beach. We had struck the beach full-tilt, end-on. The tide was falling. Tides always do in accidents. We let ourselves down upon the beach and took our axes with us, and then, by lantern light, went on a search for posts, and found small trees, and cut them of the lengths we needed. We posted the *Sonora* up. The tide left her high and dry. She rested well upon her posts.

And now we saw how wonderful was our escape. All sorts of ugly rocks and boulders lay piled and scattered on that beach. Our steamer's planks were old and rotted. A moderate blow upon them would have smashed a hole. Yet the *Sonora* by luck had driven up the beach squarely, had struck with her solid steel-shod keel, had nosed between two rounded boulders that had lost their balance easily and fallen apart. There was no damage done. We floated when the tide came up, and went upon our way.

The *Sonora* had, long ago, lost most of the metal "shoe" upon her keel. Her rudder worked upon a post that came down from the deck above and had no bar of metal, continuing the line of the keel, to keep it rigid (in the water) at the lower end. The missing piece of metal shoe had served this purpose.

Now it happened one night that in passing we had to put in to the raft at Hanson Island for some freight. There was a sou'-easter blowing across Western Channel full upon the raft—full blast— gust following gust incessantly. So we had some difficulty, after we had loaded freight, in getting clear from the raft in the teeth of the wind, and in the end we went off in a curve. We passed near to the point of rocks that makes one head of the little bay, and began to turn into our proper course in the free water at the mouth of the narrow Twofold Passage that opens there into Western Channel.

The wind was tearing down the Passage, gusts slatting down from off the mountain, jostling one another, shaking the poor old *Sonora*. Just then there came a sudden queer easiness, a quiet absence of resistance, in the steering gear. The turning of the wheel, too, seemed to govern the boat's movements even less than usual. I thought at first it was the *Sonora*'s habitual submissiveness to wind. Then I realised that the rudder had dropped off . . .

The night was villainously dark, the hour about midnight. The *Sonora* blew down the Passage, plaything of wind and swift-running tide. She blew sideways, broadside to the gusts, lying across the narrow channel. At first we thought to make our escape back into the wider waters of Western Channel. We had three men on board, and two rowboats towing astern. We took one line from the bow upwind to a rowboat, another line to another boat downwind from the stern, and by hard rowing in the boats tried to twist the *Sonora* to point up-channel. But the gusts mocked our efforts.

Then we realised that safety lay in keeping the *Sonora* crosswise to the channel. When in the darkness we could hear the wave-noise on the rocks close by our bows we could back out into the channel. When noises were made close to our stern we could give the engines a few revolutions forward. We took the old chart down into the engine room. The chart was half effaced; the light was dim. Was that mark upon the waters of Twofold Passage put there to show a rock? or was it a mere fly-blow? We strained our eyes to see; we had never been there in a steamboat before, and we had not heard of any rocks. We decided that there was no rock. Next day we learned that we were wrong. The ugly rock lay in mid-channel.

The *Sonora*, however, did not hit this rock. We blew sideways down the Passage, zigzagging from the shores, in the black midnight; beaten upon by rain and the sou'-easter. We blew at length into wider waters, steamed behind an island out of the wind, and dropped anchor hurriedly in a patch of fathomable water that the chart told us of. Next day we rigged a huge rough-hewn sweep over the stern by way of rudder, and a sloop motorboat from the hotel towed us triumphantly to Port Browning.

"Quite an escape we had last night," said Bill, and thought of other things. Accidents were all in the day's work with the *Sonora*.

# CHAPTER XX

# Steam and the "Sonora"

N EVER YOU GET behind the donk when she's working," said
the youthful engineer to me; "that cylinder head when it
blows away like that might take a man's legs clean off." But I did not
need the warning.

Carter's old donkey-engine was a mechanical chimera, and yet
perhaps no worse than many others in the Western woods. The
work it had to do was, of course, severe. The hauling of a blunder-
ing, lumbering log of huge size and enormous weight through all the
obstacles and pitfalls of the woods; the sudden shivering shocks to
the machine when the log jams behind a solid stump or rock and the
hauling cable tautens with a vicious jolt; the jarring, whirring throb
when the engineer hauls in the cable with a run to try to jerk the
sullen log over some hindrance — all this puts a great strain upon
the soundest engine. The strain of such work upon Carter's en-
feebled rattle-trap was appalling. The whole mechanism would rock
and quiver upon its heavy sleigh; its different parts would seem to
sway and slew, each after its own manner; steam would squirt from
every joint. The struggling monster within seemed always upon the
very point of bursting from his fragile metal covering. In moments
of momentary rest between the signals from the woods, the engineer would sprawl over his machine with swift intensity. Spanner in
hand, he would keep tightening nuts that would keep loosening; it
was a never-ending task. Hauling would often be interrupted, too,

for more serious repairs. But still it was wonderful what the machinery would stand. One way or another the donkey did its work, and that was all that Carter cared.

Shovelling coal in the bunkers of a liner had been the job nearest to Steam and machinery that I had ever held before I stepped on board the *Sonora.* I had read newspapers, however—accounts of explosions and boiler-room fatalities—and I had in consequence all sorts of queer, limited ideas. I soon learned, aboard the *Sonora,* to take a wider view.

I learned that Steam was a most mild and harmless thing. So the men, for instance, who became scared on board the *Wanderer* and left her in a storm in mid-channel on Coola Inlet (and never set eyes on her again) must have been as children, afraid of their own shadow. Then I saw how silly was the story that they told of the *Dovecote's* engineer—the story that he dived overboard sometimes when the engine had made queer noises. And I kept an open mind about a vague yarn concerning a Dutchman near Alert Bay. It was said that he had been found scalded and the engine room in some disorder. I learned that as long as a man did not let the water get "too low" in the boiler, and as long as he had "any savvy to him" and did not lose his head "if anything happened," that there was "no trick at all" in handling the engines of a decrepit steamboat.

Suppose, for example, on the *Sonora,* that the condensers suddenly "bucked on you," and the cylinder head was then liable to blow off. I knew that you reached up to the second set screw on a medium-sized pipe on the left-hand side of the engines and turned it. Then the steam would go into the exhaust or some other convenient place. Anyhow the cylinder head would cease, I understand, to yearn to be a rocket, and you could fall to pondering as to what on earth might be the matter with the disobliging condensers.

I hate to tell you all about the *Sonora,* because she was so humorous, and you will think I am piling it on, drawing the long-bow. Sometimes when I used to look out of the pilot house at the gaunt, gloomy cliffs and mountain slopes of the Inlet and think how it would be if anything really serious did happen to the *Sonora*—

sometimes I used to wish she had been less of a jest, less like the curate's egg.

Higgs and I had met her the previous summer when we were on a sloop, cruising for timber leases. She came into sight round the head of Tooya Cove (where we were anchored) one misty morning, a blistered, dingy, disorderly junk slowly sighing her way through the water. Listening intently, you could just hear the faint throb of her engine, that was like the heartbeat of a dying man. You kept expecting it to die away and stop.

Two months afterwards I boarded her with my blankets and bag at Port Browning, on my way up to Carter's camp. Bill was getting up steam. The young fellow that owns the *Gipsy* was in the engine room discussing with Bill ways of straightening out the rod of the pump. Someone had hit it a blow when heaving cordwood into the fire. They fixed it somehow.

I was a passenger that trip, and I sat on the stern writing a sentimental letter. We oozed out of the harbour, the engines going jink-jonk, jink-jonk in a wavering manner. They sounded quite loud when you were on board.

Suddenly steam swirled in clouds out of the engine-room doors. Burning billets of wood hurtled out, into the water overboard. Then Bill shot out and ran forward. The *Sonora* began an immediate ominous circle back to Port Browning. I realised that something had happened. It was a mere nothing, however. After a few attempts, Bill managed to get near enough to turn some valve or other and stop the escape of steam. It then appeared that about a foot of the injector piping had blown away. We continued our voyage . . .

The *Sonora* was the second tug built on the B.C. coast, the pride, thirty or forty years ago, of the Westminster Steamship Company. One day, in tidying up, among the pile of cartridge boxes and empty bottles, and Bill's town clothes and receipts, and duns from Vancouver tradesmen, and undelivered letters that rests upon the shelf over Bill's bunk in the pilot house—I discovered a picture frame, under the glass of which was a faded certificate, which read as follows—

| | *Sept.* 2, 1901 |
|---|---|
| **s.s.** *Sonora* | |
| Length . . . . . | 54 feet |
| Gross tonnage . . . . | 33 tons |
| Register tonnage . . . | 18 tons |
| Nominal horse-power . . | 4·2 |
| Boiler : Maximum pressure of steam } permitted } | 80 lbs. |
| (Signed)  J. K. JONES, | |
| | *Inspector.* |

I did not know myself what these figures about tonnage and horse-power meant; nor did Bill. He said that someone told him the *Sonora* was of 36 horse-power; two engines of 18 horse-power each. Anyhow we had the satisfaction of knowing that six years ago a boiler inspector had been confident that an 80-lb. pressure of steam was quite safe. We always used 80 lbs.

Since 1901 the *Sonora* had lived a secluded life up various inlets. No inspectors had vented their prejudice upon her, nor meddled with the safety valve. That class of person, I understood, was too much trodden down "by appearances." A man ought to be free to exercise his own judgment, and if *he* knew that machinery and boat would *do* the work he required them to do, what on earth did it matter how they *looked*? . . . Bill spoke quite warmly on the subject.

When Bill would achieve his full head of steam, his 80 lbs. of pressure, the *Sonora* would go full-tilt, perhaps six miles an hour. The whole boat would quake in a sort of palsy. The engines would palpitate—jiggety-jiggety—klink—konk—very quick. We would ourselves catch the cheerful infection and become lively. But this mood would never last. A new sound would begin to enter into the full chords of the engine harmony. Something would begin to hammer and bang, and soon Bill would stop the engines, and we would drift at random while he and I worked with spanners, tightening this, loosening that, shoving little bits of tin into joints, nursing the engines back to sanity.

That engine room was a fine warm place in cold weather, when a man's wet feet were numb with standing in the icy pilot house. The sliding doors opened on a level with the outside deck. One of them was usually kept open, to let out the smoke that escaped through the cracks in the plaster, plugged upon holes in the furnace. You would put your leg through this door and go down a little ladder to the engine-room floor, about five feet below. There you would stand in warmth, warming hands and cold feet before the cracked doors of the furnace. Behind you were the jiggling engines; cylinders covered with disreputable jackets of asbestos plaster (that looked like the dusty peeling plaster of a disused cellar); mouldy-looking brass machinery; rust-eaten, discoloured pipes, tied up here and there (at joints or at holes) with rags held by clamps. Steam would be squirting out of one or two places, that Bill would be intending to fix next time he should have the chance. Chips of wood and the ground-up powder of dry fir bark would be littering the engine-room floor, but these, now and again, would be swept up with the remains of a broom and thrown into the fire with something that had been a shovel. There was nothing *new* to jar upon you in the *Sonora*. Everything was in keeping—harmonious, antique. Bill even used an axe with a split handle to break up the great slabs of bark; and he wore, with unconscious good taste, a torn shirt, engine-greasy, and trousers rent in the seat. He had a large assortment of more or less broken tools to tinker the *Sonora* with; and in every cranny and on every shelf of the engine room were odds and ends of supplies, spare parts, metal things that "might be useful," bits of pipe, old tins, and every broken fragment that had been taken out of the *Sonora*'s machinery for ten years past. Behind the engine room, but on a level with the deck, there was the tiny cookhouse, that held a stove (that by stifled smouldering would cook a tepid meal), a shelf to eat at, and boxes for men's seats. Neither Bill nor I would bother much about the cooking. Syrup and ship's biscuits and corn-meal porridge were good enough. The cookhouse stove discouraged us. Behind the cookhouse was the bunkhouse—the cabin, as you would say. Inside there were two bunks, two berths; and narrow lockers on which, also, men might sleep.

Pilot house, engine room, cookhouse, and bunkhouse made, as it were, one building. Besides this building there ran, upon each side, a narrow deck, some three feet wide, fenced in by tiny bulwarks. This deck was usually piled high with firewood—with long billets, with big slabs of fir bark, each many inches thick. The deck around the stern held other piles of wood.

A little iron ladder took you up to the house's roof, alongside the tall, slim funnel. There lay our axes, and a big falling saw, and sledgehammers, and steel wedges, and metal-shod springboards, for our use in getting fuel. And a huge frayed tow-line was coiled up there; and there was a rack of lanterns, of glasses red and green and white. The lanterns may possibly have been usable. We did not know: we travelled without lights.

*Hand-loggers coaxing a log: rolling it over with screws and barking it.*

# CHAPTER XXI

# Hard Times Coming

T HE SONORA LAY anchored in Port Browning, awaiting Bill's return. Rumour of depression had sent him hasting to Vancouver, to sell logs at whatever price he could. For Carter was short of money, and in a logging camp some ready money you must have. Men working for you may choose to leave at any moment. You tell them airily to "get their time" at once from Bill; you pay them cash; they go. Woe to your vanity, woe to your credit at the stores, should you lack the necessary means. For men will talk; storekeepers and saloon men, creditors, will learn about your state; the tangle of your affairs will soon be made insolvency.

The *Cassiar* came to Port Browning from Vancouver trip after trip, and Bill did not return. At last he wrote:

THE BODEGA HOTEL
AMERICAN PLAN
VANCOUVER B.C.

MR. GRAINGER DEAR SIR, — I have tried all over to sell the logs and no sawmill will look at them i never saw times as hard as they are now they lend money at 25 per cent some are paying sixty and glad to get it at that the mills cannot get money from the banks to buy logs one mill has shut down no money to pay their men. On the American side the banks have no money at all business men here cannot tell whether times are going to get better or worse it is a

panic. you may expect me soon as i can get some money I hardly
know what to do i know they are short of grub up at the camp but
they will get along some how. There are lots of broke men in town
now all the camps are shutting down and the sawmills may do so to i
could hire good men as low as 2½ dollars per day. It is hard times
and no mistake

> yrs truly
>
> W. ALLEN

Between the lines I could read of the tottering fortunes of Carter
and Allen, tottering through no fault of theirs, shaken by some
tremor of the New York money-quake; and of Bill doing his disheart-
ened best to shore those fortunes up. Bill, all these days, would be
drifting round Vancouver offices and hotels, trying and failing to get
his business done, with borrowable money every day becoming
scarcer. Like other master loggers, he had no accounts to show, no
evidence of his solvency; Carter never minded books. Bill must try
to borrow money where he had so often loaned it in more prosperous times; by aid of the mild, quiet esteem in which men held
him. For everyone liked Bill — open-handed, squandering Bill, who
could never refuse a friend a loan. Carter counted on this popularity, having none himself to use . . .

Waiting in Port Browning, I heard other news of bad times
approaching. Men arriving from Vancouver talked of a strange difficulty in finding work after a happy holiday in town. They brought
newspapers with them that told of a poor crop in Manitoba, of a
shortage of money there, and of the currency crisis in the States that
was rolling dense vapour clouds of depression over Canada. British
Columbia lumber, it was said, had ceased to sell in the Northwest;
the sawmills could not even get their pay for lumber sold. The
outlook became most gloomy to men in Port Browning; loggers and
hand-loggers with half-completed booms in the water. They brooded
as they worked . . .

Over at the hotel the talk of lounging men was gloomy. Camps
all around the district were shutting down. Going to Vancouver, the
*Cassiar* was packed with men. And yet what use to go to town?

Of the shortage of money queer yarns were told. For instance, a man spending a few days on the American side had put his wad of money safe in a Seattle bank. His visit ended, he went to draw his money out. "No cash paid out from here," the bank had said. "Here, however, is our acknowledgment; payment, we hope, will not be many months delayed." In Seattle things were so bad, we heard, that men paying for their drinks in dollar bills would get the change in writing — bartender's script!

Money, as yet, was plentiful enough at Port Browning Hotel; men were still spending their recent wages. Of an evening, when darkness had driven me from my work of cutting steamer fuel, I used to row across to the hotel, or to the store, watching and talking to the boys. I never had a cent myself to spend; yet visiting the hotel meant accepting drinks every few minutes. I would figure in introductions, "Captain of the *Sonora*"; and my new friend would say, "Pleased to make your acquaintance, boy; comeandavadrink!" I would watch the card game; Bob Doherty perhaps on the win. Bob would be setting up the drinks, paying for meals for anyone around who was short of money, supplying one or two special friends with counters for the game. "Had your dinner in the restaurant?" he would ask hospitably.

I saw some thrilling fights. French Pete and Nobel had a great set-to one evening, both being sober, in settlement of some deep grudge. Fifteen minutes it lasted in the barroom; none of your "scraps" — hit, grapple, go-to-the-floor-and-bite affairs — but a proper stand-up fist fight, an unusual thing.

There were games too. Players would arm themselves with slats of boxwood, half a dollar would be placed upon the barroom floor, and the game begin.

A man, confidently swift, would rush to pick the money up. To reach the floor he must bend; bending, he would present a curved behind; terrific smacks of boxwood slats would be delivered there. The man would spring upright, reeling, with a yelp. The rest of us would roar. So the game would go on, in bustling style, with wonderful good temper — until boxwood would run short.

It was strange to take a last look at the lively, rowdy scene — the fiddler, the groups of men, the red-hot stove, the coloured whisky-dealers' pictures, the brilliant lamplight shining through strong wire masks, the dazzling altar of the bar—and then to step outside and seek your boat. Gee-wiz! but the weather would be cold and fierce sometimes. I would get my boat baled, wait a moment for a bad gust of wind to pass, and then row, at full strength perhaps, towards the lantern light aboard the *Sonora*. Squalls, lashing, tearing; rain, sleeting, dashing in your face; snow maybe; utter darkness; utter winter weather . . .

But empty pockets and distaste for drink made me prefer the quiet store to that disorderly hotel for an evening visit. There we were sedate, sitting on the counter or on boxes round the stove, engaged for the most part as listeners to conversations. The latest news from Vancouver would be heard and debated. Some man fresh from cruising timber on Queen Charlotte Islands might tell about his trip. Are there two metals, alu*mini*um and a*lu*minum?—a high debate.

Dave Felton might tell the boys of his approaching trip back home to Wisconsin, on money made by selling timber claims last summer; dandy Dave Felton, passing round a tailor's receipted bill for a hundred-dollar suit of clothes! Or the stormy weather and disasters caused might bring us back to our staple subject—logs. Two million feet of logs had broken loose at the mouth of the Nimpkish River. "Now I'll just show you the mistake that company made," says someone, and draws with a piece of chalk upon the floor. "They had their boom hung across from here to here. What they oughter have done was to . . ." Amey, a master logger working some miles up-coast in Johnstone's Straits (that rough water), came in one evening fresh from a catastrophe. We heard the simply told story: Amey's anxiety at the weather; the tug that came to his aid, too late; the breaking of his boom; the four hundred logs that floated away to sea; near two thousand dollars lost—a sore blow to a small contractor.

A few days after, Dutchie the hand-logger came to seek a helper. Hundreds of logs had been floating past the little bay where Dutchie had his boom. He had gone out, towed in log after log, filled his boom. He had worked right on for fifty hours, he said, until he had dropped exhausted. He had caught two hundred logs. Then the weather had got worse, and Dutchie had sat upon a headland watching a wealth of logs that jostled in the sea and passed to and fro before his bay with the ebb and flow of the tide.

Then talk would turn, perhaps, upon some recent accident. I remember M'Carty telling us how the log had slipped and caught Pete's boot and rolled upon him, and pushed his body before it down to water; and how Pete's arm alone stuck up above the surface. "Squashed he was, flat, like a squashed fruit, from his ribs down," said M'Carty sadly. Similar accidents would be recalled, and then we would talk of the hospital and the mission ship and its good work; and what was wrong with missionaries; and how set women, and some men, were on religion — and what a rum thing that was. Then it would be time for me to light my lantern and go out into the rain and row to the *Sonora* and to bed. Down the harbour anxious searchlights would be flickering where half a dozen tugs had lain, this week and more, anchored in shelter from the raging weather in the Straits; tugs moored to huge, long rafts of logs, watching to steal their way south to Vancouver sawmills.

On Tuesday and on Friday nights, however, my sleep would not last long. Perhaps at midnight, perhaps at two or three o'clock, the siren of the *Cassiar* would sound from down the harbour and wake me with its echoes. Then I would jump from out my blankets, put on my boots, and light a lantern, and row hurriedly through the darkness to the warehouse raft to see if Bill was coming back from town. Then the glare of the searchlight from the *Cassiar* would light up all the water, and show the raft and the hotel and Mitchell's store in turn. Boatloads of men would come out from the shore. Soon the *Cassiar* would tie up at the raft, opening a big doorway in her side for the discharge of freight and mail-bags. Passengers would jump off. Then blankets and bundles would be passed up, and men would climb aboard, and after a few minutes the *Cassiar* would give a toot and loosen her rope and go off down the bay, Vancouver-wards, while we would row our boats away, and tie them up, and go to bed again.

Sometimes the *Cassiar* would take another kind of passenger. There would be helped aboard, perhaps, a man limping with a foot all bundled up—chopped by his axe, most probably. Or a mattress would be lifted in by careful hands, and on the mattress one would see a man lying helpless, his broken leg rough-bandaged. Some of these injured men would have been brought long distances, in open boats, delayed maybe by stormy weather.

"You bet it ain't no dressmaker's dream, getting hurt so far away from any doctor," said a man to me once; and I have known men to avoid the northern camps for that very reason. Unpleasant, to get badly hurt, without antiseptics, bandages, skill or knowledge of the proper care of wounds, four or five or six days' journey (weather permitting) from a hospital!

I stood upon the raft one night talking to the purser of the *Cassiar,* asking him for news of Bill. The light streamed on me from the open doorway of the cargo room, and I was in the way of people entering. Suddenly someone behind me called out "Gangway!" meaning that I should move aside. A queer thing happened . . .

There must be *tones* still in the dulled human voice—primeval tones, tones used of old by human animals before the words of speech had come. For example, shouts of "Help!" may merely excite your quick attention, or they may spring you to the rescue, spasm-struck, according to the tone. There was a *tone* in that word "Gangway!" Hearing it, I did not need to look behind me. I *knew,* without seeing, what was there!

I stepped aside, and watched five men advance to put some piece of freight aboard the steamer. "Gently!" said someone . . . it was a great big box . . . it was the hand-logger killed the day before in Western Channel, hit by a falling tree. I rememberd, then, that someone had told me of the accident. A quiet-looking man, cleaned up for town in rough black woollen clothes, followed the box on board—the dead man's partner. I fell to wondering what part of earth that hand-logger had come from, and whether his relations would ever know that he was dead. The quiet suddenness, the simpleness of the death of healthy men! I had a choke in my throat, rowing home.

CHAPTER XXII

# Living on the "Sonora"
# at Port Browning

THE SONORA LAY at Port Browning, Bill still delayed in town.
I had found, in the lagoon behind the islands, an abandoned
log that hand-loggers had cut back in the woods and worked down to
the beach and then had found streaked with rot—a log worth cutting up for steamer fuel. Forty feet long it was, and four feet through
at the smaller end; over four thousand feet of board within it; worth,
had it been sound, from five to eight pounds sterling according to
the market price.

On this log I worked daily, in the rain, sawing it into four-foot
lengths. These lengths I had to split into billets; billets that, stacked
upon the beach, were fuel for future voyages of the *Sonora*.

Daily, about dark, the rain would come heavier, in deluge, and
gusts of wind would come tearing through the trees, making a be-
lated worker feel lonesome, making him think of warmth and dinner. So I would launch the skiff and row toward the distant lights of
the hotel, near which the *Sonora* was anchored; the skiff, unwieldy,
turning circles in the wind, blowing across the harbour. Patient
work it was, reaching the *Sonora*. Then I would persuade the damaged cookhouse stove to burn, to cook a meal, and go below and
bale the steamboat with a bucket (one hundred bucketfuls), and
then find drier clothes and sit at ease eating and warming myself
over the smoking stove, avoiding as I could the drippings from the
leaky roof. Sometimes I would have visitors.

I found a strange boat astern one evening when I returned

aboard. In the cabin, wrapped in Bill's blankets, lay a man, a stranger whose face I half remembered seeing at the hotel. He was awake, eyeing me, coolly unconcerned to see me enter; he made my anger rise. But it proved to be an ordinary matter. The man had felt the horrors coming on and had fled the hotel, taking refuge on the *Sonora,* as far as he could get from whisky. He was, one might say, oozing with a hysteria that he could just manage to control; the horrors can seldom get a grip upon these healthy men. Bromide and a meal or two and quiet were all he needed: a day or two later he left Port Browning on his way to work. A case like this, of a kind so often met with, shows one how decent boarding-houses would abolish half the harm of drink. Hotels are now the only stopping places for travelling or idle men; barrooms the only places where they may sit and wait; whisky a distraction that is simply forced upon them. A man has no fair chance.

Another evening, Ed Anderson put his head in at the cabin door and "chewed the rag" with me awhile, on his way aboard the ancient, mouldy steamboat *Burt,* that he and Smith and Dan Macdonnell had raised from where she last had sunk (in shallow water). "I don't see that a woman would be anyways uncomfortable living up in these parts," said I, thinking of the problems of my own affairs. "Here's a feller been writing to me that no decent woman could live near a logging camp. He ought to know, because he lives in a big town called London — not London, Ontario, but London in the Old Country. There is only decent women living in them English towns, you know." Ed grinned; his notion of a town was different. He chewed, and considered.

"Naw," he said — "NAW! I'll tell you, feller. There's a rough class of people in this country here — a rough class of people. And there's not a one of 'em 'ud fail in respect to a lady" (lady=woman; Ed had never heard of class distinctions). "Not a Blank-Blank One" (emphatically). "You can't say the same of many classes of men," he reflected.

One afternoon I saw the little steamer *Gipsy* come tearing up the harbour and make a dashing landing at the warehouse raft, under the critical eyes of the crowd on the hotel veranda. "Ma" was steering: Ma steers and cooks for Pa and Herbert, who hand-log somewhere up Call Creek and use the *Gipsy* for towing logs. A jolly little bandbox of a boat, the *Gipsy*; 35 feet long, with newish boiler, steam-pipes the thickness of your little finger, cylinder that would go inside a large silk hat; bought, a bargain, for 800 dollars. I went aboard that evening, and sat in the clean living room of the pilot house and held discussion with old M'Kay. I find it hard to believe that so effective a worker should be over eighty years of age: wonderful old man! He was a Canadian volunteer in the American Civil War; he served in the United States Navy; he came to the Pacific Coast in '68 and joined some rush for gold in Cariboo. He gave me anecdotes of a friend of his, a man named Rhodes, who made four fortunes, and once paid the public debt of Something County in Oregon (a matter of 160,000 dollars), and died in a poorhouse somewhere in Washington; the Governor of Oregon coming in person to fetch away the corpse for honourable burial. Then he talked of hard times he had seen, and hard times coming now. This winter would be the worst time the Coast had ever seen, he said. Most of us at Port Browning were of old M'Kay's opinion; the news from Vancouver kept getting worse and worse. I felt the situation must be very serious, for Bill was still in town, trying to get money. He did not even write to me.

What on earth would Carter be thinking, up at the camp? Three weeks ago the cookhouse had been short of grub, and Carter had expected us to return within a week, bringing a new supply. Unless the boys had had good luck in shooting deer and goat, the camp would be starved out by now. So every time I saw a rowboat rounding the far point of shore outside Port Browning I would stop work and watch — to see if it was Carter coming, in fury at the *Sonora's* delay...

One day a boat came into sight — several men in her, one man baling. It was our rowboat, come from Carter's camp; it made a bee-line, hurrying to the hotel. That evening Ben Morris came aboard the *Sonora*, finding me at my supper. He gave me the news from camp. "We came down the Inlet just a-whizzing," he said (his breath a form of whisky), "howling north wind behind us; showed it a foot of our sail; had to take shelter once or twice. *Say!* Mart! Carter is talking pretty free about you fellows. What'yer been doing, staying here so long? Carter's near starved out. Fitz and me and most of the other boys kind of got weary of that ruddy country up there. Wish we'd known times was getting so bad on the Coast; wish we'd stayed at Carter's camp, now! Well, guess I must be getting back to the ho-tel. Fitz is good and drunk and gone to bed; most of the other boys are pretty full. There's a card game on and lots of booze. Come along! Well, good night!"

When Fitz and Ben Morris had sobered up I invited them to live on board the *Sonora,* Fitz being a great friend of mine. One night Ben came home late, after we had gone to bed. We heard him tie his boat astern. Then he opened the cabin door noisily and began to stumble down the steps. He was "good and drunk." Fitz felt that my hospitality was being abused; an old grudge, besides, began to rankle. Without inquiry, without remonstrance, without asking or provoking the least word from Ben, Fitz, from his bunk in the black darkness of the cabin, of a sudden began to talk. At the first word Ben stiffened and ceased to move, listening; there was something worth listening to. It was not rhetoric, nor violence of swear-words, nor abuse. It was just the miracle of a plain man inspired (by some happy chance) to tell in simple words his very thoughts. Fitz spoke slowly, reflectively, in an easy, subdued voice. He sketched Ben's character; he weighed Ben's moral worth, and found it a poor thing, wanting. As for the actions of a hobo like Ben, they were naturally those proper to inferior men ... Fitz had been saddened by the knowledge that a man like Ben lived in his logging country. I lay awake; I would have given anything to have had that speech in writing. It was of the very essence of true oratory: simple, elegant, unanswerable.

He ceased to talk and there was silence — a long silence. Then the staggered Ben pulled himself together and jumped outside the dark cabin. He had been stunned by what had been said, by what had been implied. The reaction was furious; he shrieked:

"You —! you —! you —! come outside here and fight."

He used *the* unpardonable expression that is in itself a command to "scrap." I thought it time to awake.

"Hullo, Ben," said I, yawning loud and stretching, "what's up?" My friendly tone stopped him a little. "G'wan," said Fitz, "g'home and go to bed." Ben howled again, "come and fight" the song. "G'wan and be ashamed," said Fitz, and rolled over to his sleep.

Ben rowed ashore, and then returned to shriek insults from his rowboat, and rowed ashore again and shouted from the beach, hysterical. We laughed till we were weary.

"This comes from being good to that sort of dirt," moralised my friend; "he's been treated good both by you and me, and he comes here and acts like that." So good-tempered is Fitz where many another man would have given way, weakly, to silly violence.

# CHAPTER XXIII

# Voyaging Between Hotels

I AWOKE ONE MORNING to a sound of swearing, and looking out, I saw the *Prospector*. A shanty, you might call it, built upon a sailboat hull; a steamboat, now, some twenty-five feet long. Engines and bark fuel and drunken Swedish captain were stacked inside the shanty; but my old acquaintance Jim leaned from the door and gripped the bulwark of the *Sonora*.

"Give us some packing for the engines, Mart," he whined tenderly; "we're getting this'yer steamer ready for sea. Sold her to an Australian feller this morning for a hundred dollars. You might oblige us, Mart!"

Jim, I know not why, was sober . . .

The big sloop motorboat from Hanson Island Hotel was lying by the warehouse raft. I watched her as I cooked my breakfast; she seemed in difficulties. There was water in her cylinders, I heard, after breakfast, when her engineer rowed over to ask my aid. Fifty dollars he offered if I would tow his boat home with the *Sonora*, an easy day's work, he said.

"Fourteen miles' towing, the labour of getting fuel, fourteen miles' return trip in the dark," I said; "and I suppose you know my knowledge of steam is about four weeks old?"

"Why, *that's* all right," he said, smiling at my amiable self-depreciation.

So I took on the job, and got up steam. A young man from the sloop came aboard to steer for me. We hoisted anchor and steamed up the harbour to where our tow awaited us. We took the sloop right square amidships, and dented in a plank—luckily above the water-line. My young steersman observed the scene with so great a calm-ness that I thought good to take the wheel myself, for the journey; and I rowed ashore and hired the still sober Jim to run the engines in my place. Jim had once worked aboard the *Sonora,* and knew the weak places in her machinery. Besides, he was the only engineer that I could find.

We made our two successfully; we tied the *Sonora* to the Hanson Island landing-stage. Jim went ashore to get a meal. It was about three of the afternoon. I was desperately anxious to get through the narrow place in Western Channel before dark, on our return jour-ney to Port Browning. So I fell feverishly to searching along the rocky shore; chopping tree limbs, splitting driftwood, chipping bark off logs—anything for fuel! At last, weary and furious, I went to see what Jim was doing. I found him in a crowded room, talking and waiting for his meal. He excused his idleness in a wheedling voice: "I'm faint with hunger, boy! *I'll* help you by-and-by. Just you wait till I've had something to eat, Mart! There ain't no hurry anyway." He showed his Cockney origin. As I left the room, the Dohertys and Ed Anderson made true apologies. They were coming with me to Port Browning on the *Sonora,* they said, and they knew they ought to be helping to get wood, but until they had had their supper they felt too weak to work. They had rowed, down the Inlet, thirty miles since breakfast.

Now working in mines and logging camps out West, a man will slowly learn a sort of tacit etiquette that Western working-men observe, often, one to the other. In the logger, for example, you may discover some punctilio—punctilio that one never hears de-fined in words. Listen to a logger yarning, telling about some epi-sode in some man's life. At any moment you may be puzzled by some touch of the quaint, the unexpected, in the way the man is said to have acted; something you fail to see sufficient reason for in the story. Question the man who tells the yarn, and you learn, from his surprise, that actions that strike you as strangely unnecessary have been related by him with unconscious gusto.

Take, for a poor example, something I heard about a man named Groves. Groves hired on as "second faller" to work at Jenkins' camp, and Jenkins put him to fell timber with Finnerty. Next day Finnerty walked into the office, asked for "his time," was paid off, left. Jenkins took no interest in this matter of routine. He put Groves with Oregon. Next day Oregon sloped into the office, asked for his time, was paid off. Curiosity overcame the good manners of the boss. "Why on earth are you quitting, Oregon?" he asked. You may imagine Oregon looking at him with lack-lustre eyes, listless and bored by Jenkins and his question. He drawled, "Oh, well, guess I'm going to town." Then Jenkins put Groves with Simmons and hid near where the pair were working. He watched them pulling the great long falling-saw to and fro, to and fro, as they stood, high in air, on narrow springboards projecting from the tree. And then he saw that Simmons was mad with the man Groves, whose heavy hands were making the saw pull hard, who was turning work to drudgery, who was spoiling the record, hurting the jaunty vanity, of a swift and clever "faller." Then Jenkins understood why the other men had gone away, and in a dim way I understand it, too, myself; but I have hinted at the reasons with a crude lack of subtlety.

That afternoon at Hanson Island I burned with fury as I observed similar punctilios of rigid self-respect. Jim should have been helping me, getting wood. He sat idle in the hotel instead. I could resort to violence, you say. Who, then, would help me engineer the *Sonora*? Short of violence I should figure undignified, weakly querulous, should I upbraid a fellow worker with not doing his "fair share of work." Decency prescribed my only course of action. I must do Jim's share of work for him, let him find it done, heap coals of fire silently upon his vanity; act the perfect logger — with utter foolishness. For beery Jim had long since lost his vanity.

So it happened that my fuel was put aboard and stacked in the *Sonora*'s engine room, that steam was up to 80 lbs. and squirting from every usual joint, and that the *Sonora* was cast loose and ready to put out before Jim and the Dohertys and Ed Anderson, and a following of other men, came aboard. Then I pushed off with a pole, jangled the engine-room bell, and away we went, jinketty-jonk, into the blackness of the night . . .

I opened all the pilot-house windows and leaned out as I steered, straining to glimpse the line where the black shore slopes and their black shadows met. Steering down Western Channel in the dark used to make me sweat all down my back with apprehension. For I have no proper Western confidence to make me oblivious of my lack of skill; and, if you wish to know, a long old tugboat may be by no means easy to steer, in pitch darkness, in a swirling tide in a channel that narrows appallingly near Low Island, where Jimmy Hill once rammed us on the rocks. Suppose, after a dozen indecisions, you gain a hope that your course is keeping midway down the channel. You pay attention to where the steamer's bow is going. Then with a start you find the stern is swinging near that shallow place on the starboard bank that shows up slightly whitish against the forest background. Next you think yourself at the proper safe distance from the starboard bank, and suddenly the tide swings you, in appearance, nearly aground upon the port. Oh, horrible channel! wherein you can see nothing safe but the shine of the water near around the bows; wherein all else is blackness: blackness that looks like shadow but proves solid — hills and shore; blackness that looks solid but that of a sudden flits away over the water and joins the blackness, and then comes solid black again elsewhere — shadows on the sea surface. Which is which, and where are you, and what room have you to swing? You wish you had a lantern hung from the bow near the water, to shine up the passing shores and give you certainty.

Some such thoughts were in my head as we went down Western Channel, nearing the narrow place. And then I realised our passengers.

Any man could travel on the *Sonora* going to wherever we were going to ourselves; Bill and I would never mind. But we used to avoid making trips from one hotel to the other, lest many drunks should come aboard. Drunks are a nuisance on a boat.

Now, as I steered, bottles were poked at me in the darkness and friendly voices insisted that I should drink. Five men were sitting in the pilot house; all had bottles, all were fairly drunk. One man stood beside me and was sober. He discussed the channel, the darkness, the difficulties of my task of steering. He breathed of the desire to

take the wheel himself. His name was Charlie Ross. Through the
partition I could listen to the noises of my engineer at work; he
seemed still on the hither side of drunkenness. Aft I could hear
shouting and happy babel. Men, I imagined, filled the cookhouse
and the cabin. I trembled for my blankets.

Soon we were in the narrow place, and I craned and used the
corners of my eyes, and spun the wheel, watching the swing of the
stern, watching the bows, watching the unseen line of shore. At my
elbow Charlie Ross was agitated; he craned and watched, and startled me with what he saw. He gave me advice; he became impor-
tunate that I should do the right thing that he said; at last he
snapped, "For God's sake PORT!" and placed his hand upon my
sleeve — the gesture of a clergyman reproving erring youth.

Now I was ruffled, because I had had enough of that sort of thing
on my first two trips, and because I lack the gift of discouraging
impertinence by a right manner. So, there being room, I spun the
wheel for starboard, *hard,* to sicken Charlie Ross. I let my elbow
catch him in the ribs — by way of accident and hint, lest I should
have to fall upon him. There was a queer noise; the wheel turned
slack. The starboard steering gear had broken . . .

Luckily the briskness of the wind had gone, there was but little
breeze; luckily, too, we could run out into the widening channel,
steering with the unbroken gear to port. Out there I stopped the
engines, and we drifted, amid black shadow — to a noise of singing
from the cabin aft.

We were so used to accidents on the *Sonora* that no one seemed
to take much interest in our plight. The most of us, drunk or semi-
sober, had a restful feeling that something would be done by some-
body to get the steamer safely to Port Browning; and even should
she bump her rotten self on rocks and sink, that everyone would
scramble ashore somehow and somewhere. Why worry — take a
drink!

Passing aft with Charlie Ross, I saw into the engine room,
where, amid the scattered fragments of our fuel supply, two men lay
warming themselves by the furnace, their hats jammed low upon
their noses, their hands waving before each other's faces, in drowsy,

guttural debate. Passing the cookhouse, I saw the soles of boots upright upon the door-sill. Lying upon the thrown-down plates and pans and kitchen outfit, the man who wore them snored convulsively, his head turned to one side. I reached in and took his broken lantern and threw it overboard, then walked aft to the cabin. It was filled with men, some sleeping (one rolled, the swine! in *my* blankets), some sitting on the berths, legs dangling, watching Ed and Billy Doherty, who were holding a lantern through a trap-door in the floor to light the cursing Jim below. Jim was the only man aboard who knew, off-hand, where to find the break; by luck, he felt alarm, drink notwithstanding, and showed us what was wrong. We tied up the break with someone's blanket rope.

So, soon after midnight, we rather lamely made our way to anchorage at Port Browning; Jim, in the engine room, cursing noisily because I took away the tins of lantern oil with which he had begun to feed the furnace. You may imagine, if you like, my feelings as I steered those last few miles, racing against Time. Our fuel was burnt to the last stick; our engineer was at the last gasp of consciousness before our voyage was over. The anchor dropped, I helped to throw dead-drunks into a rowboat; I said good night to other men; and then I was alone, looking with rueful eyes into my smashed-up kitchen. Never again should drunks be let travel on the *Sonora*, I said, and fell to nursing my uneasy vanity, dissatisfied with the figure I myself had cut among that drunken crowd. You note, perhaps, the limitations of my character displayed so artlessly before your reading eyes. You smile at what you see. And what would you have done yourself? Used the hard fist? Tipped someone overboard? Brought violence among that happy, rowdy crowd of drunks?

CHAPTER XXIV

# Dan Macdonnell

D AN MACDONNELL WAS a quiet, steady man; big-chested,
active, cheerful, like the better sort of bluejacket. He was a
master of the Western art of makeshift — the art of rough-and-ready
and never-at-a-loss — that does not worry if the proper tools are
lacking; that will at need make, without fuss, bricks without straw;
improvising the "good-enough" that *proves to be* good enough.
When bad times made Ellerson shut down his camp, Dan (who had
been blacksmith there) drew a fat cheque and moved over to Port
Browning and lived in the hotel. He did not booze; he did not waste
his money. Once in a while he would join the boys for a few drinks;
but no one ever saw Dan drunk. Not that he was anyways a *mean*
man, you understand. All that was just Dan's way.

Now, the previous summer a decrepit old steamboat named the
*Burt* had ventured up the Inlet. The men who owned her meant to
hand-log up round Tooya Cove, using the *Burt* each night to tow
their new-cut logs to shelter. But the *Burt* went aground the first
night at high tide, and tipped over at low, and filled and sank when
the next tide came. They had a great job raising her, and all their
grub was spoiled by the sea-water, and so they gave up hand-logging and left the district, losing about one thousand dollars. The
*Burt* was left anchored in Port Browning in charge of Bullfrog Todd.
Todd got drunk one day. The *Burt* tipped and sank again, just
opposite the hotel.

Ed Anderson was loafing at Port Browning then. He did not seek work; he had no money; but there was a boom of logs up in Wah-shi-las Bay in which he had an interest. It was not saleable in these hard times; but it gave him standing, and he could trade upon the fact of its existence—for meals and liquor. Wise-looking, ease-loving, experienced Ed Anderson!

Bullfrog Todd when sober made furious lamentation, finding the *Burt* had sunk. He preached one of his great sermons, standing on a chair in the barroom, amid an uproar of applause. "I blame myself, I blame the drink, I blame this blank-blank whisky-hell," he chose as text, and made one feel that politics had lost in losing Todd. Sprawl-ing, fat, noisy, drunken Bullfrog Todd! They say he is a splendid engineer.

*In the evening.*

I do not know what queer intentions brought the three men together — Dan and Ed and Bullfrog Todd. I know they joined, a company, in raising the sunken *Burt*. They floated her successfully; they cleaned out her machinery. Soon I was annoyed to see them cutting up a log I had meant to use myself; they were getting fuel for a voyage on board the *Burt*. Dan Macdonnell had bought the necessary grub and engine-room supplies. The *Burt* was to be taken cruising round the Islands and in the Straits, picking up and towing floating logs — beach-combing.

One day I got up steam on board the *Sonora* and (a friend steering) took her down the harbour to a little creek where steamboats often go to fill their tanks. Late in the afternoon there came a sudden mist, filling Port Browning. We crept back cautiously to the usual anchorage, shadows guiding us. Just before I meant to stop the engines something in them clicked and broke. We anchored then. Early next morning I went to where the *Burt* was anchored to seek the help of Bullfrog Todd. He, it seems, had been on a furious "bust"; he was all drink-bleary and haggard, his hands shaking. But he came and saw my engines. "Get a blacksmith," he advised.

"Who'll I get?" said I.

"Dan Macdonnell's your man," said Todd; and I rowed him back aboard the *Burt*.

Now it is not difficult to find a man you want to see in such a place as Port Browning. You try the barroom first, then take a look around the rocks near the hotel, then look at faces in the beds upstairs. That failing, you row over to the store and make inquiry. Your man not being there, you row across to Felton's shack, and stop at Ben the Englishman's, and then row up to Pete's.

I did all this. I did not find my man. Dan Macdonnell was not at Port Browning! Then where the deuce was he?

Later that morning my friend Mitchell, the owner of the store, came rowing up to where I worked. "Come and row down the harbour with me," he shouted. "Charlie Leigh's gasoline [motorboat] came in just now, and Charlie says he could see a boat ashore below the bluffs. He thinks it's some boat that's drifted there."

Mitchell was a man who felt responsibility, as our leading citizen and postmaster. Moreover, in this case it was clear that *someone* would have to go and rescue the stranded boat and keep it till the owner should appear. So I and Mitchell rowed down the harbour to the place that Charlie Leigh had spoken of. There we found, at high-tide mark, just underneath the boughs of trees, resting comfortably among the rocks, undamaged — the *rowboat of the Burt*!

And Dan Macdonnell no one ever saw again. He had dropped, that sturdy man, into infinity; he had vanished from our world. You see his name before you on this page. That is now all I know of that Dan has left behind.

Just for the moment, when Mitchell and I returned to the hotel, Dan's disappearance roused a general interest. Jem the bartender, good-hearted little man, at once took out a search party, and cross-examined Ed and Todd. Mitchell went over to his store and wrote a letter to Vancouver to the police; he hoped they would send someone, some time, to Port Browning to report. Then we had our dinner, long after it was due . . .

We had to hurry over eating; darkness was not far off, and we had certain work to do. For there was a pig upon the warehouse raft, in a big cage. The steamer *Cassiar* had left it there for Revellor, who had a ranch on Galiano Island. The wretched pig was getting sick for want of exercise, and Mitchell, after dinner, asked some men from the hotel to help him raft the huge fat animal ashore. So there was great shouting — and fun. Side-splitting laughter shook us when a man, old Spot, fell in the sea and stood waist-deep, too drunk to get ashore. The pig was landed and all the dogs collected, and there was a pig-hunt and several dogfights. Mitchell of course put up the drinks for everyone, by way of thanks for their assistance. Then we watched the boys rollicking along the beach and round the house — a lively scene. Mitchell stood silent; then suddenly he said to me, "He was a damned decent fellow." It was, I guessed, Dan's epitaph.

# CHAPTER XXV

# Last Voyage and Sinking of the "Sonora"

T HE WIND SEEMED very fickle as we wound our way among the islets of the narrow channel; it came in flaws and gusts, from here, from there; cutting the tops of wavelets into small driving showers of spray, rattling the broken windows of the pilot house. We knew a strong sou'-easter must be blowing down the open Inlet.

Bill came up to discuss plans. The engines were working *good,* he said; there was lots of wood aboard; we had the big skiff towing astern, and not the rotten rowboat. The skiff was buoyant and did not leak. Besides, our new way of towing her, with the *Sonora*'s hawser (as thick as a man's arm) looped right round under her keel and lashed with good strong rope, would guarantee her safety. Therefore, Bill thought, we should pay no attention to the weather.

It was dark before we turned into the Inlet, from the end of Western Channel. We caught the first shock of wave. We began to pitch. Fortunately our course was head-on to the sea.

Coming further from behind the land, we met the wind — real sou'-easter and no mistake. The *Sonora* bumped and bashed into the waves, rude horseplay for a poor old tug. Spray smashed at the pilot house and drenched me, as I steered, through the shattered windows. There was a high, whining noise of wind in the ropes that stayed the tall funnel; we might, for the sound of it, have been an ocean liner.

Through the thin partition behind me I could hear the babel-racket from the engine room, where Bill was tinkering with fevered hands, his dear machines all a-rattle and a-bump. Slam, jingle, clank!

There would be a moment's breathless pause. Then the screw would race—the whole ship shivering, to set your teeth on edge. Then there would be a noise of fire-rake, and Bill could be heard hurling wood into the furnace. The hurried way he would slam the furnace doors told me everything. I could picture him, sweating with a very proper impatience, flying back to nurse his engines with a spanner; listening to mutterings and hammerings with discriminating ear; tightening nuts that were coming loose; keeping a wary eye on this and that; persuading the time-eaten machinery to miracles of cohesion.

The skiff, towing behind in the darkness, could take its chance! I could not leave the wheel; Bill could not leave the engine room. We could do no good to the skiff, anyway, in such a sea. The hawser would hold, even were the skiff to swamp; and after passing the mouth of Sergeant's Passage, where the tide rip danced with high-pointed waves, the sea had come steadily from ahead, and a following boat was in some shelter.

About two in the morning Bill came into the pilot house.

"Nice weather for a rowboat trip!" We grinned to one another in the darkness.

"Nice weather for us," said Bill resentfully; "here we aren't up to Boulder Point yet—not ten miles in eight hours! I've got to be firing all the time to keep up any steam; we've used up a terrible lot of wood. We ain't got enough wood to go on bucking this wind up to Sallie Point, that's sure."

Now, in this sou'-east wind Boulder Point anchorage was no earthly use to us. We hated to turn back and run for Protection Point. Bill said Andy Horne had told him once that there was anchorage in a little pocket of a bay that you would hardly notice, passing, just beyond Boulder Point.

We decided to go and see—a hateful job to me, for I loathed strange harbours and narrow waters. The *Sonora* was such a brute to steer, and backing, would not answer her helm. Besides, her captain was not skilful.

We reached the place; we had luck; we sidled into the very centre of the tiny dark bay. The anchor held; there was no wind.

It was five o'clock on Wednesday morning. We had been a-work since Sunday morning, sleeping four hours on Monday night, while sleepy passengers had steered and stoked. Now we stumbled into the *Sonora's* bunkhouse, by a last effort removed our boots, and fell into our blankets. Sleep extinguished us.

We awoke some time in the afternoon. The *Sonora* was riding close to shore — so close that we might have thrown our axes into the mossy rocks. Splintered wood, in tangles, lay among the big drift-logs on the narrow beach; and we marked a fallen tree with bark that looked easy to loosen; and there was a pile of rejected stove wood beside a roofless cabin. Hand-loggers or trappers must have lived there once. After eating we made two journeys with the skiff, filling her each time with a great load of wood and bark. We looked out on the Inlet, and the wind seemed no longer so furious. About nightfall we hoisted anchor, backed our way zigzag to the open sea, and continued our voyage.

The wind was blowing steady, no trouble to us. But alas! something very definite was wrong with the engines. Something *pounded* — pounded hard — something that was not used to pound before. We knew so many rhythms, so many notes of the music of our engine room. This sound, oh hark! was new.

Bill slowed the engines down: we crawled along hour after hour, with frequent stops to test the usefulness of some new idea, some way of dealing with the damaged engine. So it happened that daylight had come, long since, before we saw the head of the Inlet and ran to our usual anchorage, a mile below the camp. We took our usual soundings; held the *Sonora* on and off, until we had found the exact edge of the "drop-off" — where the river flats of the Kleen-a-Kleen go steep to the Inlet's bottom. We dropped our anchor and tested its hold. Anchoring at the head of the Inlet was quite an affair!

Bill, by now, had guessed the cause of the pounding in our engines. A key, a sort of little metal wedge that should have been jammed tight into an iron casting, had got worn and loose. We spent a day in taking the engines to pieces, in carrying the casting and its companion piece up to the blacksmith shop at the camp, and in forging and fitting a new and excellent key. Bill it was who gave the finishing stroke to the job. He drove the key home with such enthusiasm that the priceless casting broke. The *Sonora*, for all purposes of movement upon the Inlet, was now a useless log upon the water! There we were at our camp with a broken-down steamboat, the boat with which we kept open communication with the world. Port Browning was over seventy miles away; a new casting could only be bought in Vancouver. As for the old one, it was doubtful if our tools could mend it. Like two guilty schoolboys, we wondered what Carter would say.

By supper-time, however, the weather occupied all men's thoughts. It was snowing in very clouds when the wind began to blow from down the Inlet, gusty and fierce; blowing, an unusual thing, into our little bay. Carter was uneasy, for his logs. Indeed, there was risk of loss; waves were breaking in spray all along the edge of the boom, thrusting the line of logs about, straining the boom-chains. Within, the carpet of floating logs heaved up and down upon the swell. The camp buildings, on these rafts, swung to the movement. They cracked; we thought they might slew over and collapse. Our rowboat, tied outside the boom, could be seen in the breaking waves that banged it against the chain of outer logs. I watched to see it smash. But Bill did not. He went walking over the heaving, grinding logs with elegant balance, sprang into the boat, and rowed it away to shelter; an action that, to look at, seemed of some merit. Soon after Bill's return the squalls ceased suddenly and the night fell calm . . .

Next morning all hands were working ashore, on the rigging. Carter was desperate, as usual. "Them logs must be got out before more snow comes," he trumpeted.

So he took Bill up the hillside to work signals for him; and me he put to split wood and act as fireman to the donkey-engine on the beach. Thus it happened that I worked all day in sight of the *Sonora*. She lay much nearer to the shore than she ought to have done, closer than we had anchored her. Evidently the storm of the previous evening had made her drag anchor. But Bill and Carter reckoned she was all right, good enough. "No time to bother with her today," said Carter; "we got to get them logs out right now." So the *Sonora* lay at her new anchorage all day; and at dark I saw her still there.

After supper Bill went down to see if the *Sonora* wanted baling. Carter and I sat in the office. He was at peace. He planned new buildings. I did the "figuring," calculating quantities of planking needed, and the expense, and calling my results. It was, by-the-bye, Christmas Eve.

Bill came in, shut the door, and sat himself wearily by the stove. Carter and I went on with Carter's amusement. There came a pause.

"Well, there's another two thousand dollars gone to hell," remarked Bill.

Carter started. "What's that?" he said, his eyes swift, glaring at Bill.

"She's gone," said Bill, and chewed his quid.

There was silence — silence for minutes and minutes.

Poor fellow! Crass and "wicked" as Carter might be, here he was, sore-stricken by bitter Fate. Bill too!

Figure the case of these two men who, by years of exhausting effort, by denial of pleasure, disregard of comfort, had won their way out of the ranks of thriftless wage-men. They had become men of substance; possessors of a small sufficient fortune; winners of success; employers of others. All had been gathered by them in fields that disaster hedged. They had laboured and succeeded and had thought themselves secure. Soon they would have had each his joy: Carter, some business in which men buy and sell; Bill, a little, well-stocked ranch, safety, and peace.

But the cold wind of hard times — the hardest ever known upon the Coast — had blown upon them. Their fortune, of a sudden, had shrivelled in the cold. And then came, oh malicious Fate! the loss of the *Sonora*, interfering with their work, spoiling their plans. They had no ready money: no fault of theirs. Money seemed to have vanished from all the Coast. Here had been the *Sonora,* a ready, useful asset; an easy thing to borrow money on — and there might be desperate need of borrowed money, to avert the loss of all.

Besides, the *Sonora* meant two thousand dollars of hard-earned money. Hard earned!

Carter, who had "beaten his brains out" getting logs off that disheartening sidehill! Carter, cursed of every man who had felt his oppressions—for this!... We sat in the office, silent. There was no noise in the world outside. Only the quiet murmur of men talking in the bunkhouse came to us.

Then Carter spoke.

"I knowed we oughter have taken her up the slough," he said.

Allen chewed.

Carter said: "She can't lie in very deep water."

Then Carter got his idea.

"We might take the donkey-engine down the beach," he said reflectively, "and take the main-line and tangle it round the boat... then haul her to shore... under water..."

He fell to considering the details of plans.

It was admirably met, I thought—that vicious stroke of fortune. I said so to Bill.

He looked up with sudden surprise.

"Why?" he said—"why? What's the use of worrying when a thing has happened?"

I guess he was right. I lost two pairs of boots and an axe in that damned steamer myself.

# CHAPTER XXVI

# Christmas Day

A FTER THE FIRST surprise and burst of talk the evening in the bunkhouse became like any other evening. We men kept a big fire in the stove, and hung up our boots and turned our drying clothes; and lay, between whiles, in our bunks smoking and spitting and thinking. The only difference was that Carter and Allen came and sat with us in the bunkhouse, and in their presence our manner was subdued to show sympathy; for we were sorry for them in a tepid sort of way, and we had not lost many things ourselves in the sunken steamer. And so the evening passed—Christmas Eve, if you please, beloved of magazine story-writers for the dramatic things that happen upon it.

When the Chinaman's gong went for breakfast next morning Carter went out and took a look at the weather. It was snowing fairly hard; we wondered whether Carter would want us to work or not. But the loss of the steamer must have taken starch out of his spirit, for he ate breakfast slowly and then returned to the warmth of the bunkhouse, and made no sign of work. Allen and others of us took the rowboat and went down the coast to the *Sonora*'s usual anchorage, and prodded for her in the water with a pole; a vain, dispiriting occupation in falling snow, on Christmas Day, with its faint suggestion of holiday. Even Allen lost interest after a while and turned the boat towards camp. We passed the rest of the day loafing in the bunkhouse, contented to be warm and in shelter from the snow.

It was after supper before Carter's mind began to work. He fell to figuring how much grub he needed to finish the logging of the claim, and how he could get it up the Inlet now that the steamboat was not running. Flour and bacon and other things would add up to one thousand pounds in weight, he concluded, and he lay back upon his bunk silent awhile—and I saw his decision was made. Then he began talking to himself, to be overheard; a long, rambling talk that would bring up now at this point—the need for grub—and now at that—the grub lying ready at Port Browning, eighty miles away. Then he would deal with other matters, fluting variations on the tune. He would stop now and then and hold debate with himself, shrewdly, carefully. But always he would come back to the two subjects—the grub for the camp that *must* be got, the grub at Port Browning that *could* be got. Then he fell to praising the Inlet: how fools exaggerate; how the Inlet was far from being a son of a dog of a place; how suited it was, after all, to voyages in a rowboat. He himself had once made the trip to Port Browning in twenty-four hours; and it made no difference even supposing the trip *had* been made in summer and *with* a fair summer wind. A trip in winter weather might take a longer *time*, but what of that? The Inlet was all right; he was only sorry that being obliged to look after the work at the camp prevented him from going down to fetch that grub himself—in a rowboat. He would do that. He would think nothing of a little trip like that. Yah! who but a frightened fool *would* think anything of it?

All this, of course, was aimed either at Bill or at me.

Bill was plainly the more useful man at the camp. My heart went into my boots as I realised that I was the person who was to make that rowboat trip to Port Browning by himself. I hate isolation. To set out alone on a long trip makes me feel like the small child who, lingering behind, screams from fear of being abandoned; or like the squadron horse, on scouting work, that frets to get back to the other horses. Nearly always, in rough journeys, one has a companion, a partner; and a partner means safety and cheerfulness and the surety of proper camps and fires and meals. A lonely man, panting to get to his journey's end, pushes on too hard, tires himself, travels too late

into the falling dusk, and is exhausted as he makes camp. Making
camp by oneself in bad weather, in a bad country, is a dismal thing
to look forward to. As Carter talked my mind pictured, in nightmare
hues, the upper reaches of the Inlet: the gloomy lowering roof of
clouds, hanging across the water; the steep-to shores, black walls of
cliff streaked and splashed with dreary whiteness of snow; the dark,
quiet sea; and the ever-present threat of storm, a threat almost
visible to the eyes in that scene of misery. That was the Inlet at
peace—unstable peace—the peace of a few short hours. Then
there was the Inlet disturbed: the cloud mass dragging past the
mountain slopes, tailing wisps of mist; the sea all ridged with the
white tops of waves in the path of a wind slanting from cliff to cliff
across the bends of the Inlet. How depressing the thought of pulling
a heavy boat with tired muscles; vainly seeking shelter from the
swell of the sea in curve after curve of the rocky shore. And darkness
coming on, perhaps, and no sign of an anchorage for the boat, and
no sign of dry wood or camping place.

"I suppose you'll want *me* to go?" I asked Carter at last, meeting
the inevitable with what grace I could. Carter gave, as it were, a
start of surprise.

"Well, now," he said, "that's quite an idea! I hadn't thought of
sending anybody. I wouldn't have liked to have asked you, boy; it's
kind of a tough trip to ask a man to take in winter." And he began
hurriedly to make my arrangements, keeping me on the run, so to
speak, showing how easily every difficulty that occurred to me could
be overcome or ignored.

"Keep moving night and day; never stop while the weather
holds good," said Carter. I thought of that sodden log of an eighteen-
foot boat, so heavy to pull. Oh, the weary hours of rowing! Keep
a-moving indeed!

"What bothers me is how I'm going to keep that boat safe at
nights if I have to stop," said I; "she's too heavy to haul up, and
there's damn few places anyway where a boat *can* be hauled up."
The rise and fall of the tide is fifteen feet on the Inlet.

"Wait till high tide and haul her what you can, and then sleep till
the tide comes up to her again," said Carter. "If there ain't no

beach, anchor and sleep in her." Delightful thought! Sleeping in wet clothes across the thwarts of a leaking boat; rising to bale her every hour or so; creeping into wet blankets beneath a dripping sailcloth; kicking aching cold feet against the kitchen box to warm them; eating meals of sodden bread, cold to the stomach. Ugh! The wait-for-the-tide scheme for me, in spite of the delays it would mean!

"That boat leaks like a sieve; she wants fixing," I said.

"Fixing! Why, I put some new planks in her last month," said Carter; "she's *no business to leak*. What do I fix a boat for if you men are going to knock her all to pieces? That boat is *all right*." Carter had never been in her; he spoke with conviction.

"When that thousand pounds of freight is in her she'll be down in the water, to her top board," said I; "how about bad weather? how about a small breeze?"

"You'll just have to lay up when there's any wind, that's all," said Carter; "you'll have to wait for calm weather. Never get it? Don't you believe that. I don't care if it is only calm once in every few days, for a few hours. Take your time, boy. Take two weeks, three weeks. *I* don't care if it takes you a month. Just work your way up little by little."

"That freight will get all spoiled, lying in an open boat for weeks; what with water leaking in, and waves splashing in, and rain and snow," said I.

"Well, it's your business to see it isn't spoiled," said Carter; "that's what I'm sending you for. You'll have to take all that freight ashore every time you stop, and pile it good and keep it well covered. And you'll have to keep the boat well baled."

I must confess I felt like telling Carter that he could go and fetch his own damned freight, and that I would see him in hell before I would do it. But I said nothing.

Shall I tell you that I was a little sorry for Carter and Allen struggling in the wreck of their hard-earned fortunes; or shall I say that I did not like to disoblige Carter? Or shall I be franker and tell of more serious motives: that I did not like to appear scared of that beastly trip, and that, not knowing the thoughts of other men, I was

dead afraid that, should I protest or ask for a companion, Carter
might get some other man to go and triumph over my mortified
vanity? The journey down the Inlet in an empty boat was no great
matter. How could I tell but that the return journey, heavy laden,
might not appear an affair of easy achievement to some other man in
the camp. Such a journey in summer would give one small anxiety.
Was not my courage depressed by the mere wintry *appearance* of
things? That is the worst of a small-boat trip; there is nothing definite to go by. One's fears may be a matter of moonshine, or they may
be caused by sound common sense. One may boggle at some adventure that the men of the country have found to be of prosaic safety;
one may think of possible accidents that are known never to happen;
and all this consciousness of the dark, unlikely side of things, of
trivial chances of danger, may be mere indulgence in shameful
nervousness, like that of a railway passenger who should hesitate to
take an express.

So for moments during that Christmas evening I persuaded my
unwilling fear to leave me. But it would spring upon me again at
some turning in my thoughts; and I would see that unwieldy boat
damaged in a dozen possible ways, and myself ashore on the rocks of
a mountainside, wet and cold, with no matches and no fuel — rescue
of my remains the affair of a search party a month or six weeks
thence. Would they trouble to search? I wondered; and I fell asleep
wishing that *I* knew less about the rottenness of that old boat, and
that other people knew more. And in my sleep I had a numb,
stomach-achy feeling like a man under shell-fire; and I was dread-
fully unhappy.

# CHAPTER XXVII

# A Ghost Story

T HE NOISE OF Carter stamping his feet into wet boots woke
Bill and me next morning. It was still dark outside, as we
noticed when Carter opened the door. We heard him jumping his
way ashore, the spikes of his logging boots making little crunching
noises on the floating logs. He was off, the first of men at work, to
light the fire in the donkey-engine. I felt dismal: I felt like Execu-
tion Morning in Newgate.

"A rotten ruddy trip for a man to make by himself," I said to Bill.

"Why, we're *both* going," said he. "We'll take the big skiff; two
men can handle her and she don't leak. There's *no sense* in one man
going; he'll take all winter getting that freight up here."

Happiness burst on me. Bill was coming; the trip would be
splendid; no horror of loneliness to be feared! But—Carter had
spoken, and who was Bill to alter Carter's word? Bill was Carter's
partner, Carter's slave. I saw how it would be, and went sadly in to
breakfast.

Carter and I stood by the bunkhouse door. "Shall we get that
boat fixed up this morning?" said I. "Then I can have a sleep and
start down this evening, and get through them windy canyons beyond Axe Point by daylight tomorrow before the wind comes up."

Carter looked across me. "I'll fix her for you," he said; and
stalked away over the boom to where the boat was tied. The boat
was full of snow. Carter shovelled some of it out, and trod down the
rest. She had taken considerable water. Carter baled it out. "She's

ready for you," he called; "tumble in your traps and get started right away. The weather's good." It was not; the slight swell told of a wind blowing away down by Anwati.

But Carter was magnificent! The dramatic vigour of his actions, the very wave of his hand, contrived to put me in the most ridiculous light should I try to protest. Protest would sound so pitifully feeble in face of such convinced, competent ignorance. Carter had forced my hand, had rushed me, in a superbly efficient way. My only chance was to get angry and violent; and I never felt less like violence in my life. I was fascinated by his charming brutality, by the way he ignored *my* convenience, by the utterly unnoticed sacrifice of *my* interests to his necessities . . . and I could only grin. The brute! He played that scene so well that I chuckle still in recalling it. And yet the boat leaked at all times; and when weight was put in her and some of her upper boards became submerged she used to leak like a sieve! It was one man's work then to keep her afloat by force of baling.

"Don't you never drive no nails into any boat of mine," said Carter as he saw me go to a nail-keg. So I took a hammer and plenty of nails; and took one of Carter's blankets (for a sail); and a tarpaulin for the freight; and a heavy piece of metal for a stern anchor; and Carter's best ropes, long ones; and all my dry clothes rolled in my blankets. Then from the cookhouse I took deer meat and bacon and tea, and all the bread that was made (to save campfire bakery), and plenty sugar and oatmeal and matches and baking powder. Twenty-five pounds of flour in the boat gave me a feeling of security; and I took a sharp axe, and a big bucket and a small tin for baling, and two cooking pots and a plate and a spoon. Finally I found a precious piece of pitch wood that the cook had hidden, and took some kindling wood for fires (in that sodden wet country), and soon was rowing down the Inlet with my eyes on the distant camp. Then I turned the first point and was alone — upon my journey . . .

There was no wind. I dreaded wind — at least the sou'-easter, the probable wind, the headwind. But a gentle swell was coming up the Inlet, and beyond Axe Point I could see disturbance in the clouds, and trouble seemed to be awaiting me ahead. I baled the

boat, and then settled myself on my seat and rowed steadily, with
the restraint of a man who knows he has to support the exertion for
hours and hours ahead, and who knows he must keep reserve
power, in case of surprise by bad weather, for a struggle to shelter.
I listened to the noise of the rowlocks, and looked at the swirls my
oars made in the water, and guessed how far I had come, and
wondered at the desperate slowness of my progress. The boat was
water-soaked and heavy as lead in the pulling; and besides, as a
steamboat man, I had become used to rather greater speeds. A
hard-earned three miles an hour fretted me; and then — oh, where
should I be when darkness should come, and where, oh where,
should I camp? To the devil with Carter's day-and-night journey.
I should like to see him, a man alone, go on for twenty-four hours
lugging at home-made oars in a boat that dragged like a barge!
I began to glow with anger against Carter . . . But just then sadness
fell upon me; a breeze began to ruffle the water. And soon the
breeze was wind, and soon ripples became waves, and waves began
to whiten and break; and the short, surfy seas hurried one after the
other, row after row, and storm was beginning to sweep the whole
width of the Inlet. I was well out from the near shore, and there was
no shelter anywhere along it that I could see. But someone had told
me once that Old Village was out of the wind, and there was Old
Village — straight across, on the far shore of the Inlet. And now from
which wind was Old Village a shelter? The north, the west, the
sou'-easter? A sou'-easter was blowing. Old Village looked good
enough; I turned the boat, angling across, deferent to the seas. A
miserable business it was, to my mind, tossing and wallowing across
two miles of channel; the heavy boat responding to my hardest work
by slow forward lurches that stopped dead at the bash of every
alternate wave; and wind and sea increasing in uncomfortable power.
But the time came when a headland shut off the wind direct, and I
rowed on gently heaving water to the mouth of a little river, and saw
good anchorage and camping ground.

It was still early in the afternoon, but there was no hope of the
wind dropping that day. I found a flat place just above the shore
rocks, and cleared away the snow. "Firewood!" Carter had said in

derision. "Fancy a man worrying about firewood in this country!"
And you might have sniggered at the thought, looking at the forest
slopes and the driftwood jammed in the rocks, and the fallen timber
everywhere. But the Inlet is cleft deep among mountains, and little
sunshine can come to dry the slopes, and rain falls for all the winter
months, or snow. So all wood is wet, and dead timber soon becomes
moss-covered and soggy; and there are few parts of the world where
a campfire is harder to light, in wintertime.

I cursed Carter as I dug my axe into log after log and found them
all rotten; and every pole and even every twig seemed rotten too.
And at that twinge of despair the horror of loneliness came upon
me, and I looked up the mountain, and over the misty, white-
capped sea, and round upon the scattered tangle of fallen timber on
the mossy rocks — and the sight was dreary, the abomination of
desolation. "Curse Carter!" I thought; "I'll never come up the Inlet
again. Never! never! never! To hell with him and his freight!"

But then there were my unpaid wages of the last three months; I
couldn't afford to lose them; I should have to come back. And at the
commonplace thought I fell again to work, seeking wood; and was
soon healed of the bitterness of lonely sadness. But I was unhappy
still.

I found, in the end, dead clumps of alder thicket, and chopped
them and dragged the sticks to my camp, a pile sufficient for the
night. Then I got my stuff ashore, at the foot of a big rock, and threw
it all up on to the little flat above. The boat I moored out in deep
water, with a stern anchor. Now dusk was coming; but my camp was
nearly made.

I rolled a rotten log to the rock's edge — a back log for my fire;
and soon the long alder sticks were burning good, and my fire had a
heart. There were hemlock boughs for a fine bed in front of the long
line of fire, and a tarpaulin (for wind screen, roof, and heat reflector)
stretched on sloping poles behind me. And by dark I had had hot
supper, and my clothes had dried upon me; and by the light of the
fire I could see to mend torn garments. So I sat stitching, and the
evening passed slow.

What is it, I wonder, that starts you listening, of a sudden, during nighttime in the woods? I was sitting at my campfire, toasting warm, weary of worrying, comforted by such good shelter from the falling rain, and drowsy at my sewing. Then, with a shock, I was painfully awake, alert; my eyes on a search, my ears listening, my whole body taut and ready for swift movement. Some sound or some gleam of firelight reflected from rock or tree must have startled into activity the primeval instinct, the sense of watchfulness that lies asleep in civilised life. A new nervous system seemed to flash into brilliant action in my body.

I was amused to find myself thinking of the glowing eyes of beasts — panthers they proved to be on further thought. I have seen a panther in the zoo, and I rather fancy I have seen the footprints of panthers on river-bars, and beasts' eyes are said to glow. So it was quite easy to watch the phantom of a panther that eyed me from behind the trees and moved in little glides, creepy crawly, among the underbrush.

But I got tired of watching the panther, and he lost form and vanished. Then the noises of the world burst upon me with sudden loudness. I held my breath, straining to hear above the noise of throbbing in my ears. How absurd, I remarked, that my own effort to hear should spoil my hearing! At my self-conscious snigger the throbbing stopped. Then I could hear the rushing sough of the waves out in the open Inlet, and the gentle roaring of the creek in its narrow valley, and the occasional crash of the sea-swell against the rocks down behind my fire. There was a queer note that rose above the other noises, a sort of whir-o-o-o-o-ing and whistling in the tall trees. It seemed interesting to try to coin a word to describe the noise — noise of the dead Siwashes, I said. For the forgotten generations lay boxed in every cavity among the rocks around me; and Old Village has been avoided by the living this hundred years and more. I wondered why. I wondered would that ghostly shrieking scare a Siwash?

And then I brooded over discredited feelings that are the jest of educated men in civilised countries — feelings that exist, nevertheless, rudimentary and latent, in most reasoning people — superstitions of the aboriginal. I recalled my childish fears in the dark; and the lesser uneasiness I had often felt in the woods as a younger man; and touches of superstitious fear that had, on occasion, given edge to my vigilance as a sentry. Had I still some relic of that ghost-fear? It would be most interesting to know the truth; to see what instincts one had; to get a glimpse at one of those hidden little parts of Self that, like the bridge of one's nose, no effort of one's own will will make visible. I remembered how my nurse . . .

Something flashed behind my ear!!! My head jerked round to look. Yet, quicker than sight could work, my head was jerking back again. Through the corner of my eye on into my brain had flashed knowledge of Something Wrong, there beyond the fire. I stared hard.

Then from the very flickers of the burning logs began to rise a FACE. It rose a foot, perhaps; hovered; then flew aloft and hung in the air amid the swirling smoke. My thoughts were still working undisturbed: "How queer, *a face*! A Mongolian face, too — see the high cheekbones and the slitting eyes. Did they not say that the ancient Siwashes were of Mongolian extr—" My thoughts stopped dead; Instinct had taken charge!

I had been sitting, lounging, on the strewn hemlock boughs. Crash boughs! I was standing by the fire — nerves tingling, body light as a feather — about to fling myself at the FACE . . .

Superstitious fear? Other emotions? Alas! I was conscious of no feeling at all. But please notice that I had sprung *towards* the FACE — not *from* it. Let me wear that fact like a medal!

But certainly I heard a raucous voice bark, "WHAT'S THAT?" And if you press me I will admit the voice was mine. Let us talk of other things, lest you take smiling notice of the word I used. "*Who's* that?" I hasten to agree, would have sounded better. For the FACE was the face of a living man.

# CHAPTER XXVIII

# Race Down the Inlet

AT THE HEAD OF the Inlet there was Carter's camp—on the western shore. Half a mile down was the place where Kendall felled timber and had his tent. He was at enmity with Carter, and never came near Carter's camp. Across the Inlet were two men, Fisher and his partner, hand-loggers. On calm days we could hear the rumbling noise of the timber they shot into the sea. But they never visited our camp; they also were at enmity with Carter.

Now on Christmas Day Fisher and his partner were tempted to a decision. Their grub supply was getting low; they would be obliged, sooner or later, to make a trip to Hanson Island Hotel to get more grub for the winter months and the early spring. Why not go and fetch that grub at Christmas time, and join the festive throng at the hotel? Fisher reckoned he was about due for a drunk; he had no need to make inquiry of his partner. Business, pleasure, and the reward of virtuous months called to these men from Hanson Island. Besides, they really needed a new rowboat.

So on the afternoon of Christmas Day Fisher was busy tinkering up his ancient damaged boat. He put new pieces of plank in her, and drove in caulking where he could, and mixed up stiff dough and plastered leaks with that, and flattened out some tins and tacked them over the dough. He made her, as one might say, seaworthy. His partner roasted a goose and cooked goat meat for the journey.

It was not, however, till late the next day that they were ready to start. And of course they had no idea that the steamboat had sunk, or that I was travelling down the Inlet in a rowboat that afternoon. I had coasted down the western shore, too far away for them to see — even supposing they had looked. And when the storm had forced me to cross the Inlet to Old Village I was eight or nine miles away from them.

Towards evening they left their camp. They coasted along the eastern shore, Siwash fashion; for fear of accidents, neither man feeling much trust in the dough plasters of the boat. The curve of the eastern shore kept them well out of the way of the storm that was whitening the centre of the open Inlet; and it fell pitch-dark before they reached Old Village, so that they did not see the weather awaiting them ahead. But when they tried to round the point beyond Old Village the blast of the wind struck them full, and the waves made them fear for the boat, and they turned back into shelter and wondered what to do. That was how one of them saw a gleam from my campfire.

They rowed into the bay, hauled their light boat up beyond tide-marks, and came to seek refuge from the pelting rain at the strange fire. That was how, through a cranny of the rocks, a shaft of light from Fisher's lantern had gleamed upon my canvas shelter; and that was why Fisher's partner, climbing up the cleft of rock just behind my fire, had seemed to show a face rising from the flames. Fisher's partner was dressed in dark blue; only his face was visible in that flickering light, and his jaw was covered with stubble of beard, that left a Mongolian outline to the hairless parts. The awful look upon his face proved to be merely the expression of eyes screwed up to support the glare and the smarting pain of wood smoke from my fire. I had never seen this man before. His name was John Simpson. Think of my joy at the presence of these men, my ecstasy of joy at hearing of the journey they were upon. We would travel together!

So I welcomed Fisher and John to my camp, and we cooked another supper and sat talking, enjoying the warmth of the fire. Late in the evening they fetched their blankets from the boat, and we all slept cosily together in front of the glowing coals . . .

By morning the wind had abated. For as far as we could see the

*On Coola Inlet.*

Inlet was free of whitecaps and merely ruffled by a breeze. It was so pleasant and comfortable in camp that we hated the thought of turning out into the drizzle and wind, for long hours of rowing. But there was no help for it; we got our boats loaded; we took to the oars — Fisher finishing his after-breakfast pipe as he rowed. I myself was filled with a new anxiety. I watched the way Fisher handled his oars, to judge of his efficiency; I watched his boat, to get some idea of the pace he would go at. For I felt instinctively that Fisher and his partner would not delay their journey by waiting for me should my pace be slower than theirs; and they were two, to spell one another on the oars; and I was one, to row all the time; and their boat was light, while mine was big and heavy. I kept level with them, further from the shore, and watched. Then Fisher put his pipe away, and we came out from the shelter of the point into the wind, striking out to cross the Inlet. Fisher's boat drew ahead.

Now hand-loggers, as a rule, are like any other workingmen out West — like sailor-men, too, as far as that goes. They can often row with some effect standing up — facing forward and pushing on the oars. But they do not understand the surpassing value of a long, steady stroke, sitting down. They row with their arms, and not with their body, in the jerky, lug-at-the-finish style of the Cockney clerk on a holiday up the river.

But Fisher, some time in his life, had done some rowing for pleasure — perhaps before he deserted from the 11th U.S. Infantry; and now he was rowing to show off. I would have done that myself if I had had a better boat; but I was rowing desperately as it was — not to get left behind. My only hope was to convince Fisher by the apparent ease of my movement that the pace was a trifle slower than my usual pace, and so weary his interest in his own performance.

And while we were crossing the Inlet the little waves were in my favour; for the heavier boat held way the better. Then we came to Axe Point, and suddenly Fisher's partner was whistling and pointing. Up among the cliffs were a herd of mountain goat, staring patches of white against the dark rock. Fisher must needs stop and shoot from the boat, and declare he hit one. I baled my boat and took a thankful rest.

By now the rain had ceased, but the wind blew cold. Oh, the misery of cold, aching feet! That was the worst of rowing; it did not warm my feet. Besides, the water of many leaks splashed around my boots. Fisher had a clock with him, and as we rowed on, side by side, he would call the hours. And every hour he and John would change places. The man who had been resting would start off with a spurt, partly to warm himself, partly from high spirits, partly from a touch of annoyed vanity that I should be rowing alongside. I dreaded those spurts; they meant gruelling work for me, for I had to keep level with their boat at all costs. Once I should drop behind and lose sight of my pacemaker, I knew my own speed would slacken; and John and Fisher, looking back, would row hard to distance me, and they would pass out of sight. Then perhaps wind would come up, and they would have reached some shelter, while I, with my clumsy boat, must turn back elsewhere; and then we should be separated for good. I knew the brutes! They would dig right on to Hanson Island Hotel, and air their great selves in the barroom. "Met Mart coming down the Inlet," they would remark. "Say, boys, but we just passed him a-flying! Him keep up with us? Well, I *should* smile!"

That was how the day passed: I rowing hard, but trying to look as if I was rowing easy, trying to keep the idea of competition out of their heads, trying to bluff them; they rowing I do not know how hard — hard enough at least to make me long passionately for camp. We stopped once, to light a fire and restore feeling to our icy feet; eating a lunch the while. And at last, in darkness, with sails set to catch a following air, we made out the dim whiteness of the cliffs by Sallie Point. We rowed in to where the deserted cabin stands by the mouth of the creek, and, with utter weariness, carried our stuff ashore. Then we helped one another to haul the boats up on the welcome beach. Oh, hot supper, and warm feet, and numb, insensible sleep!

Inhabitants of houses in some London square — ordering their lives among fellow men, occupied in very thought with mankind and its milder activities — may gain the habit of regarding death and agony and natural catastrophes as mere topics of conversation. So also the traveller, to whom companions are given, may clean forget his nervous fear of the tragic face of Nature. Witness, in my own case, how a wilderness that had daunted me became the barely noticed frame to a human picture. I passed a day of tiring work, in the company of two other men, occupied by the interplay of a few childish vanities. That was all! So prosaic and so simple!

Yawnings and the creaking of the cabin floor under Frank's waking movements woke me in the dark to take my share in the breakfast work. We were short of wood, so, rather guiltily, we tore up planks of the flooring and made a good fire, for there was starlight outside and the air was bitter cold. Breakfast, besides, was that morning an important meal. We knew, inevitably, that we should push right on to Hanson Island that night, at any cost of effort. Need to fill our stomachs well; we might have to row the whole cruel distance. We hoped not; we hoped heartily for wind, now; for the Inlet turns west at Sallie Point and all winter winds are fair, going down. But when, soon after starting, our boats turned the corner point and we could see in the early dawn the long western stretch of water before us, no sign of wind was there for our encouragement. We had to row and, rowing, be victimised by vanity. So the hours passed as they had passed the day before. We rowed abreast, oar almost to oar; we quickened our pace when John changed with Fisher, or Fisher changed with John. We stopped at the same moments to bale our boats. The ache of cold feet was a daylong misery.

It was dark when we passed Protection Point, and I was in a cold sweat from weakness; my hands were sore, my wrists were numb. The other men were leaving me behind; from somewhere ahead I could hear the splash of furious baling. Suddenly arose a great shouting, that I answered, and out of the darkness Fisher's sinking boat ran alongside mine. One of the dough plasters had come out.

That was why, oh blessed relief! the great race was never finished. We reached Hanson Island Hotel in my boat, late that night; two of us rowing, one baling. And before my bed was made on the attic floor of the hotel, Fisher and John were reasonably drunk in the barroom. Glorious first drunk of the season!

# CHAPTER XXIX

# Back to Carter

THE MORNING WAS FINE and calm when I pushed off from the landing-stage and began to row slowly down Port Browning Harbour upon my homeward way. Eight days had passed since I had come down the Inlet, but during all that time rain and sleet and snow had fallen turn about, and furious sou'-east wind had blown. I had lain idle at the store, waiting for calm weather.

My boat, as I pushed heavily upon the oars that morning, moved slowly like a barge. Like a barge, too, she floated low upon the water, and like a barge she was piled high with freight. One pile filled the stern, another the forward part; between the two there was a space where I could row and bale.

The Finnish boat-builders at the Port had plugged me many of the larger leaks; the boat with all that freight in her leaked hardly more than formerly when empty. But she had lain so many years upon rough beaches, been dragged over, bumped upon, so many rocks, had so many loads of steamer fuel hurled roughly into her, that little strength was left in her worn, cracked planks. The unpainted wood, besides, was all splintery and sodden with sea-water. Sudden shock or strain, I knew, would open up the puttied seams afresh. I pictured in my mind dark landings among rocks in fear of storm, and the laden boat bumping in the swell, while wading alongside I hurried to throw the freight ashore. She would never stand that sort of thing. Such single-handed work with rotten boats was foolishness.

As I rowed—stroke upon stroke upon stroke—and watched the swirls from my oars spin slowly astern, and glided sluggishly through the still water past point after point of the forest shore, I became haunted by unhappy thoughts. To be frank—I felt fear. Fear of the boat swamping; fear of wind and waves and chill water; fear of the poignant ache of cold feet and cold hands, and cold, wet clothes; fear of rocky shores and enforced landings at the feet of cliffs; fear of freezing clothes and night, of wet snow and physical exhaustion; of the upper Inlet, where in that dismal wintry weather no tired man could ever hope to light a fire and warm himself and cook his food.

Fear ached inside me as does a rotten tooth. Mile after mile I rowed, and there was nothing to distract my mind in that monotony of movement. The shores past which I rowed were pleasing to the eye even in that winter season, but they were all familiar and monotonous; they did not hold my thoughts. There was no help anywhere; nothing to save me from picturing the shores that I should come to by-and-by *Up There*, up Coola Inlet—up among the cliffs and snow and desolation. Days and weeks perhaps of misery ahead! And loneliness!

I have a great power of frightening myself with terrors vividly imagined. When, lost among such thoughts, I woke up suddenly that day to find myself among the dancing waves of a small tide-rip, and when the boat took water over both low-sunk sides at once, I felt a spasm of a much more tolerable fear that almost gave me pleasure. I rowed hard out of the rip, half thinking that I might need to throw freight overboard. But the trifling scare eased me wonderfully in mind and stilled my worrying imagination.

So when towards evening I rowed wearily into the small bay where Hanson Island Hotel moors its many boats, I thought of nothing but my supper. I piled my freight upon the landing-stage and covered it from fear of rain, and walked up to the house.

There were a group of men upon the hotel veranda, and one of them asked as I came near:

"What the blank is the matter with your boat, feller?"

"There ain't enough time before supper to tell you all that," said I, by way of being humorous.

"She looked wonderful low in the water when you was rowing in," said someone.

"She had a wonderful amount of freight and water in her," said I.

"You don't mean to tell me you're going up the Inlet like that, Mart," said another.

"I don't like the idea," said I, with a grin that was not jaunty, upon the wrong side of my mouth.

"It's just straight suicide," said he.

Then I went in to supper feeling miserable. For I am very much affected by other people's judgment.

Talk after supper stirred my imagination. "I'll be blanked if I'll take that freight up in that boat," I said to myself; "I'll hire a gasoline, and if Carter kicks at the expense I'll pay for it myself..."

To clinch my resolution, it happened that I heard, soon after, the throbbing of a motorboat that came into the bay and anchored near the landing-stage. I waited, patient, at the barroom door until the owners of that boat had come ashore and had their first four drinks. Then I went up to them and asked if they would take me and my freight to Carter's camp. My heart beat fast at this my opportunity.

The men consulted among themselves. They felt that times were hard and dollars scarce. They knew their boat was good, their engines sound and reliable. They had no fear of breaking down among the upper reaches of the Inlet. Therefore they agreed to take my freight and tow my boat for thirty dollars, provided that they could choose their opportunity and make the trip in quiet weather.

I could have sung with joy to hear them talk; to think that the misery of that dismal trip had passed forever from me. I clinched the deal; I stood the drinks; I went upstairs and spread my blankets on the floor and went to happy sleep. And the whole hotel shook with the furious battering of gusts of wind; rain rattled loud upon the roof. A stiff sou'-easter wind was blowing.

In the small hours of the morning one of the owners of the motor-boat came and woke me up. There was a dead calm, he said; a lull between sou'-easters. There was a fine chance to get to Carter's camp before wind should arise. We took lanterns and loaded the freight into the launch cabin, and soon we put out and sped up the Inlet, towing my boat astern.

The night was very dark; dark masses of cloud hung low upon the water. But the water surface had the dark sheen of perfect calm, and there was nothing to check our utmost speed. The launch quivered as it speeded along; outside in the night the water made a rushing noise, plashing from our bows. I, who had no work to do, a passenger, lay upon the piled-up freight listening through the long hours to the whirring of the petrol engines, noise like some great sewing machine. And I thought so happily: This is my last impression of the Inlet; this my last trip among the gloomy canyons and the snow-slopes and the icy winds. When the launch should arrive at Carter's camp I would collect my boots and clothes, those ragged properties, and get my pay from Carter, and jump aboard the launch again, and shout to see the last of Coola Inlet . . .

It was about noon when the launch ran alongside Carter's boom. I went across to where Carter stood staring at us from the cookhouse door.

"And what the blank is this?" said he.

"This," said I, "is *my* racket. It don't cost *you* a cent."

Now I had not meant to take upon myself so easily the cost of hiring that launch. Perhaps in doing so I had been stung with desire to try to make Carter feel mean. But at all times I will do much to avoid haggling over money. I like to be obliging; and here, with Carter, there was distinct temptation to be quixotic. Any action which was not plainly due to sordid motives would worry Carter into puzzled thought. I used at times to do small kindnesses to him, work in his interest to the neglect of my own, perform actions that would ring true, ring of unselfish fondness. And these experiments of curiosity would pay me well in fun. They rankled in Carter's mind; they would not square with the mean theory of humanity he had formed. He felt I was manoeuvring to get the better of him; he felt baffled at such clever hiding of acquisitive intentions.

Carter called to Bill, and the two men walked away over the logs and went ashore and sat long in talk. They seemed to come to some decision. Carter took an axe and went to work where the donkey-engine stood upon the beach. Bill called me to the office.

"We're going to send away the men," he said; "times are too bad and there ain't no sale for logs, and we're up against the money trouble hard. We've got to keep expenses down and get along as best we can. We'll keep that feller François until he's worked off what he borrowed from me in Vancouver and then we'll fire him out. Carter wants to break you in to run the donkey, and then him and me and you can go on hauling logs quietly until times get better. You just see to paying off the men, and they can go down the Inlet on the launch. I'm going down myself on business to Vancouver."

I was completely disconcerted. I had been upon the point of telling Bill that I was going down myself. Now it seemed unhandsome to interfere with thought-out plans . . .

The men had been paid off, had gone aboard the launch, before I nerved myself to speak.

"How about myself, Bill?" said I. "There won't be no boats coming here, nor mail brought up. I'm just in the middle of planning to get married in the spring, and me stopping here will make a long break in letter-writing and put off getting settled. My woman won't like it either, not hearing from me. I've got to go in a couple of months anyway."

Bill went across again to talk to Carter. When he came back—

"Carter says of course you'll suit yourself," he said coldly.

"What will you fellows do?" said I.

"Don't mind about us," said he; "we'll get along all right. I guess we're going to have a good try to raise that *Sonora*."

I felt somehow as if I was leaving Bill in the lurch.

"D'you *want* me to stop?" said I.

"It would be appreciated," said he.

I thought (such is my power of imagination) that a faint note of appeal was in his voice. Then (motives are generally double) a pretty picture of Carter and Bill and I going through all the details of the manoeuvres of woodsmanship, from falling timber to hauling logs, from hauling logs to booming up, glowed for a moment in my mind and vanished. What a fine experience that would be—what a training for anyone who, like myself, had a vague idea of starting a logging business of my own some day. (Some day when I should have earned some money.)

"I'll stay," said I.

"Please yourself," said Bill, and went aboard the launch.

My chance to quit had come and gone.

# CHAPTER XXX

# Nerves and Remorse

T HAT EVENING CARTER and I sat by the cookhouse stove. François, well snubbed, had gone back to the bunkhouse, and Carter's soul was on the grill; producing an offensive odour, as I thought. Bad times, bad luck, Bill's squanderings, the sinking of the *Sonora*—all these combined to light a vicious temper in the man.

He talked of the *Sonora*—in savage, murmuring voice.

"I *paid* for that boat. I tell you I *paid*; there weren't no mortgages on her. That's nothing to *me*. *I'm* not worrying; there's no need for *anyone* to worry. Them swine at Port Browning hate me. They'll be pleased to hear she has sunk. I DON'T CARE if she has. I can *get her up* whenever I want to. I can buy a *new* boat if I want to. I can. Understand? I CAN. Answer me now? D'you hear me?...

"That donkey-engine of mine is no more use to me. D'you understand? She's wore out. I want to sell that donkey. I *can*. I can *sell* that donkey. I'm telling you. D'you hear?...

"There's no man in *this* country can show *me* how to log. I'm a *logger* and I understand all about logging. But I tell you I'm sick and tired of beating my brains out against these ruddy sidehills. These here leases wants a company with lots of capital to work them. The ground's too steep for me and the old donkey. Besides, men won't work on such sidehills."

Carter shouted, rolling his black eyes.

"I want to *sell* these leases. I want to sell the leases, and the camps and the donkey and the steamer, and the whole blank-blank

blank works. I can go and get *more*. I'm a *logger*. But what I was meant for was *buying* and *selling* . . ."

He dropped his voice and murmured. Then he began to eye me shiftily, and I thought rancorously.

"I tell you this here sentiment and obliging people is all *slop*. I KNOW. A man is working for you for just what he can get out of it for himself. If he sees he can get a dollar out of you he'll do a dollar's worth of work if he can't get it no other way. He won't do a fraction of a cent more.

"I've had experience; I know what men are. They're all the same, every mother's son of them. I've never met with gratitude or men obliging me for nothing; there ain't no such things except in talk. Men that wanted to oblige me I always found was after something for themselves on the quiet, though some was blank-blank clever in hiding it." This was a dig at me apparently. It seemed to relieve Carter's feelings and his tone became more amiable.

"I pay for all I get. I never ask for no obliging. I don't oblige nobody. I'd be the same with me own brother. *That's right!* Running a logging camp teaches you what men are. Remember Jim Hunt? He was hook-tending for me, and a first-class man he was. He came to me one morning when we was stuck—trying to get logs out of a fierce-looking gulch up on that there sidehill. I was depending on him, and he knew it.

" 'Carter,' says he, 'guess I'm going to town.'

" 'Right you are, boy,' says I; 'suits you and suits me. Get your time from Bill right away.'

"That's the way. Never show you care. I give as good as I get. Once a man quits I never coax him to stop, and I'll *see that he does quit* too. No 'changed his mind' for *me,* even if he's a man I'm really needing and can't replace. That dirt can get to blank out of *my* camp, no matter who he is, or how long he's worked for me, or what's the matter with him."

Carter's thoughts savaged him. Talk ceased to give him ease. His eye caught sight of account books lying on the table. He seized one and read inside, moving a thick guiding finger from word to word.

"Hi! whad'yer charge that Frenchman a dollar for them gloves for? You *paid* that for them. You're working for *me*; them gloves was brought up on *my* steamboat. D'you understand? Am I going to run a boat for a convenience to people, and them pay nothing towards the expense? How much would them gloves have cost that feller if he'd been obliged to go down himself and fetch them? D'you think he's going to thank you or me for saving him money? Eh? Answer me now! You've got no business get-up to you when you go doing foolish things like that. Take your book and mark him down two dollars for them gloves.

"This here's his store bill. He's had more tobacco than that; it's never been charged up to him. Put another two pounds in his bill. Don't you worry now. Let him kick if there's any mistake . . ."

Carter's talk had usually a charm for me. I could sit and listen to it by the hour; grunting in answer to his questions to show I was awake; pleased to be getting a sort of lazy knowledge of the man. But that evening Carter got upon my nerves; his talk disgusted me. I feigned sleepiness and escaped to bed.

But in my sleep a horrid shape, like Carter, pursued me with its talk and made me join it, entangled me, in never-ending work that led me even farther from my woman. Nightmare fright woke me at last.

Then, lying in the darkness, I saw myself to be a fool. I belonged again to the weakly-obliging class of men, the facile type that lends its barroom friends small sums of dollars when wife and family are going hungry. For I had imposed a two months' silence upon my woman, shut myself away from marriage plans, dropped out of sight into an uncertain world that letters could not reach—done all this injury to serve the mere convenience of Bill and Carter. For I was only a *convenience* to them; my work a trifling help towards the gaining or the saving of a few miserable dollars. I saw how childish I had been. Staying with Carter for a sentiment! I could have kicked myself. Remorse gnawed me . . .

And now began days that I would not willingly live through again—days that seemed lengthened into weeks. There were just the three of us, you understand—Carter and François and I. At the best of times we had not liked each other. Now we had to work

together, and eat together, and bear each other company, and there
was no escape from such association. And our nerves, besides, were
all on edge.

Carter was working, overworking, from mere nervous craving
for work. Work was, for him, a vicious habit, and he seethed with
anger all through each day to think how purposeless work had become. Times were too bad! Logs were unsaleable! To work and haul
logs into water was to let the sea-worms spoil the good wood! Not to
work was to go through nervous torture!

François was toiling (since he must) to pay his debt to Carter and
to earn enough money to take him "back to God's country" — anywhere away from Coola Inlet. He was a scared man, scared by the
news of hard times, scared to move from Carter's camp without
money in his pocket. There was still fresh upon his mind the memory of some mysterious "trouble" he had had with the police at
Vancouver. And so he stayed with Carter, and staying, hated Carter — hated him venomously. Crawling over the tangled, matted
wreckage of the woods, falling breast-high into piles of brush and
tree-limbs, handling heavy blocks and hooks and wire tackle in the
treacherous wet snow that covered every pitfall, slipping and stum-
bling at his irritating work, François would almost foam with hate of
the man driving him. He would come to where I worked, at every
chance, his eyes gleaming, after some new offence from Carter.

"The blank-blank son of a dog," he would gasp; "d'you know
what that blank sez to me just now? He . . ." The man would splutter.

Perhaps my own condition is revealed in this — that once when
François shook his fist at heaven and jumped upon his hat I did not
even smile. It seemed a very proper thing for him to do. I felt like
that myself.

The tide was far out, after supper, on the second evening. Across
the sands a light showed from Kendall's tent. And the idea came to
me suddenly to go and visit Kendall — that solitary hand-logger who
never came near Carter's camp. So, for the first time in all these
months, I made my way round by the beach to the little rock-strewn
point of land beside which Kendall had made his camp. A stolid sort
of man I thought that he must be. For avalanches may repeat themselves; and Cran and Blackmore had been killed by one the previous

spring within a few feet of Kendall's door, and broken timbers of their buried cabin still cocked themselves skywards from among the clay and boulders. I should have thought Kendall would have felt uneasy when wakened in the night by the hollow roar and echoes of the rock-slides that we used to hear.

Into the dizzy tropic heat of his air-tight tent Mike Kendall welcomed me with a flood of words; the sudden outpouring of a man who had not used his tongue for many days. He poked more wood into his red-hot stove and put a billy on to boil some tea, and turned his lamp wick higher, in hospitality. I sat me down upon his springy bunk, springy with fine hemlock boughs, and let my head reel as I breathed the fierce warmth of the oft-used air. It is a marvel to me that logging men, who live so much in open air, can like these hothouse atmospheres at home.

Mike's photograph, I saw, would have made the fortune of a hair-restorer. Long hair stood out all round his head and fell upon his neck as you may see in giants' portraits in children's story-books. Mike's beard was long and sweeping, his whiskers and moustache immense. He asked me, at some future visit, to bring my scissors and cut his hair.

We had tea, and Mike gave me at great length his views upon the methods used in Wall Street and upon the currency crisis that had brought hard times upon us all. Harriman had said this, Roosevelt proved that, James K. Hill had been interviewed — to fill pages upon pages of ten-cent magazines; the consolation of Mike Kendall, a lonely reader living in a hot tent among the snows and gloominess of Coola Inlet in the winter . . .

Talking was a rare enjoyment to Mike Kendall. He needed no encouragement from me. So he talked, talked well and argued (at second hand) with force; and I gave him a formal attention. But my eye wandered round the tent's interior, noting the well-kept rifle, the piled goat-skins, the ragged clothes hung up upon a line, the pan of yeast dough set to raise, the gap in the rough-hewn floor where Mike was used to split his stove wood, the clumsy table, the tins of groceries, and then the sacks of stores. Mike seemed to have very little flour left.

I almost started as an idea struck me.

"Pretty near out of grub, Mike, ain't you?" I asked, breaking in upon his talk with sudden intensity.

He said he was.

"What d'you reckon to do about it?" said I, breathless.

"I'm expecting the Doherty boys up most any day now," he drawled; "I arranged with them months ago to bring up my winter's grub."

"Mike," said I, my heart thumping with relief, "when the boys come, for Heaven's sake—*for Heaven's sake!!*—don't let them go away again without telling me. I'm just crazy for a chance to get down this blanky Inlet."

*Mike Kendall's boom.*

# CHAPTER XXXI

# I Quit

THE DOHERTYS WERE COMING! Their rowboat might come into sight, a distant speck, at any moment! So the morning after my visit to Mike Kendall I began a feverish watch-down-the-Inlet, haunted by the fear that the men would reach Kendall's tent and leave their freight and go away again (forgetting me) without my seeing them from Carter's camp.

It was part of my work to cook our hasty meals. Now as I cooked my eye was ever glancing through the window to see if any object were moving in the distant water. Once in a while I would take a hurried look through Carter's glasses.

Between meals I worked near to the beach with François, handling the rigging on the snow; Carter working the donkey-engine and running to and fro to help us. We would haul two or three logs in the day, after great efforts: a futile sort of work. And I worked listlessly, for I could watch the sea.

Carter must have been annoyed at my poor activity, for he set himself next day to gall my vanity.

"You look sick, boy," he said sweetly. "I want you to do nuthin' but cook for me and François from now on. Don't you come out to work no more. Just cook and clean up the bunkhouse, and saw wood for the stoves, and flunkey around to fill in time."

I felt sick enough. The constant strain of watching, the sudden hopes when moving specks would appear upon the Inlet's distant water, the ache of disappointment when these specks would reveal themselves as mere floating logs, the remorse that never ceased to worry me—all these had sickened me till I felt physically weak.

And my sense of humour had played out under such drain of nervous energy, and because of that Carter contrived to get the better of me. My vanity was absurdly hurt. To be cook and flunkey to Carter and François! The blood of all the Celts boiled in my veins. In a childish rage I went across again to see Mike Kendall. He counselled patience. "He's got you in a tight place, boy," said he; "don't give the man the satisfaction of seeing that you mind. Besides, it's only for a day or two. The Dohertys are bound to come soon." I felt desperate.

"Mike," said I, "I'm pretty near the end of what I can stand from Carter. If the Dohertys don't come on the third day from now, will you get out your sloop and take me down to Port Browning for thirty dollars?"

Mike looked at me in silence, doubtfully.

Then I argued with him; pointed out how we could set up his old cook-stove on the sloop, and take lots of firewood; proved to him the course that he could take in each contingency of nasty weather. The sloop was a good sea-boat; Mike could await a favourable occasion for his journey home. He could bring up his winter's grub himself and save expense.

But all my talk did not convince him. And as I walked back to Carter's camp that evening I had a guilty feeling that I had been *tempting* Mike—tempting him to break good resolutions; to run the risk of going to Port Browning, the risk of going near to whisky, the risk of going "on the bust."

In cooking I did, without conscious thought, what men are used to do when living upon a few simple foods. From meal to meal I varied the manner of cooking, varied the ingredients of cakes and puddings. So Carter saw another opening for delightful subtlety. "That *last* cook was a dandy, François," he said, at table (that I might hear); "all-ways the same, François, all-ways the same! You all-ways knew what you were going to get to eat, and just how it would taste. That cook was ALL right. Youbetcher!" Carter was discovering the gulf that lay between himself and me, a gulf whose width my sense of humour no longer bridged. François was now his confidant, taking my former place.

But all these small manoeuvrings and all the notice that I took of them were matters on the surface. Beneath them and beneath the everyday employment of our faculties, our inner selves, all three, were under heavy stress. We lived confined together under such mutual repulsion; our work was so purposeless, so unsuccessful; the days were spent in such gloom of fog and falling snow, or else in such sight of bleak mountain slopes and gaunt, snow-blotched cliffs — the whole process of our life was so dismal, so devoid of livening motive — that all three of us were suffering from nerves.

Carter showed a distinct hysteria in his treatment of his dog. That wretched animal had long fled away from Carter's touch. It lived a frightened life around the outskirts of our camp, and (as I have seen dogs do when wolves were prowling round a campfire) it was used to bristle every hair on end, and snarl and show its teeth, and slink away whenever it had come near Carter unawares. But it now happened that Carter caught the dog in the blacksmith shop, and there he first soothed it with a piece of meat, and then tied it to the anvil, and then took a stick and beat the animal till it was nearly dead. At any other time I should have felt like interfering; I could not have endured the howls of pain. But I was too much taken up by my own tortures to care the least for Carter's dog . . .

So five days passed at Carter's camp and I came near the breaking point. The morning of the sixth day I got out of bed in a nervous fury. But when I had busied myself over the cooking of the breakfast, and thumped the gong to waken the other men and summon them to eat, I felt somewhat composed. I took my place beside the cooking-stove to pour and flap the hotcakes that go swiftly from pan to table during the course of every breakfast at a logging camp.

Carter came in and sat him down, and then François. Carter, I saw, was in a villainous bad temper. He began to eat.

"Cook me two eggs," he barked suddenly.

I went to cook them without realising his tone.

"Take the lid off the stove," shouted Carter.

I felt there was something wrong.

"Turn them eggs."

It burst upon me with a rush. This was Carter's railroad foreman's manner—a manner that I had seen him use to other men!
This was the first time he had tried that manner upon me.

"Put salt and pepper on them." It was an order—staccato.

The tone cut me like a whip.

I heard his words with difficulty; the word "salt" was indistinct.
There was a throbbing in my ears. I had some idea of going closer to
him to hear the better . . .

I found myself floating towards him in a sort of atmosphere that
shook in little waves like the shimmering of air upon a plain, under a
blazing sun. I did not hear my own steps or feel my own movements. The air buoyed me up. Objects surrounding Carter, in that
cookhouse scene, were of foggy outline, blurred; and only objects
near to him were visible at all. Fog cut off the rest. It was like
looking down a tunnel. But in the middle of the tunnel, clear cut
and distinct, was Carter's face, framed in black hair and beard.

My eye caught Carter's—Carter's black beady eye.

"WHAT SAUCE?" I yelled in Carter's face.

It was touch and go. My fists were quivering for the blows;
nerves along the inside of my wrists and up my arms were itching.
I could feel a sort of succulent anticipation of the collapse of the
cranky table, the smash of the shattering crockery, the wrestle and
fall and bump as Carter's body and mine should reach the floor.
There I would bash him in the face and put an arm lock on him. A
gloating thrill ran through me to think how I would listen for the
crack of Carter's dislocated arm as the lock bent it back beyond the
natural outstretch. There would not be much moving of that arm for
Carter for the next three months or so . . .

Then Carter's eye dropped from mine, and I had a vivid picture
of a sparkling Carter looking at a sparkling plate upon the breakfast
table. Notes of mildness came to me across the vibrating air. The
noise seemed to soothe me, seemed somehow to put a sudden check
upon the spring I was about to make. I felt my whole frame relax
from a great tension—every nerve untauten, almost noisily. But

what words Carter spoke I do not know, nor even what happened
then . . .

I came to my prosaic self kneeling upon the bunkhouse floor.
I was engaged in rolling up my blankets, with movements swift and
intent. My bag had long been packed, ready for departure at any
time.

I took my bag and blanket-roll and pushed open the bunkhouse
door — and met Carter coming, face to face.

The logger quitting is a man of great punctilio. I played the
perfect logger.

"Well," said I, faultlessly correct, "guess I'm going down the
Inlet."

Carter gave me a quick look, that was an error of deportment. It
showed unfeigned surprise, for Carter based his influence over men
upon the sixty miles of Inlet that cut them off completely from the
world except when boats were plying.

"All *right*," he said; and then, "How are you going?"

"In Kendall's sloop," I said, not truthfully; for Kendall had not
given his consent.

That was an unpleasant stab for Carter — the suggestion of Kendall interfering with his policy; Kendall whom he had hated bitterly
ever since that mortifying game of cards.

Carter took my remark without the least sign of interest. "You'll
meet Bill below," he said listlessly, looking over to where the
donkey-engine awaited the day's work. His meaning was that Bill
would pay my wages.

"All right," said I, and jumped down upon the beach and clambered round the coast to Kendall's tent, with never a glance behind.
Then I remembered that my new working gloves were on the cookhouse table. Dignity forbade a return to fetch them. The value of
two dollars lost!

I came to Kendall's tent, and found the man engaged in cooking
a late breakfast. "It's no use trying to work while the snow's this
deep," said he in explanation; "I just get up when I feel like it these
winter days."

"Mike," said I, "I want to stop with you. I can't stay in the same camp with that Carter, not one moment longer. It's beyond me; I feel sure there would be some bad trouble come of it." And then I told him what had happened, and offered to pay for my board until the Doherty boys should arrive; and offered to pay for my passage to Port Browning if the boys should fail to come.

But Kendall made me welcome and put aside my offers of payment. *Of course* I could stay with him. And besides, as he told me smiling, "I'm right pleased to do anything to annoy that blanky Carter."

So I laid down upon the hemlock mattress inside the stuffy tent. And all day long I stayed inert; shaking and weak in the reaction from the extravagant emotion of the previous days; sick at the stomach, too, after the excitement of the morning. But when evening came and I had eaten some of Kendall's doughy bread and feasted off a wild goat kid that he had shot, I began to feel better. Then Kendall and I pictured to one another the state of Carter and François up there at the camp. Neither of those men could cook to satisfy even his own palate. Each loathed the other's cookery. Kendall and I laughed and giggled till we ached to think of those two enemies now forced to live and work together — to cook for one another!

Then we went to bed, and Kendall could not understand why I should want to sleep with my head against the doorstep in that air-tight tent of his.

# CHAPTER XXXII

# To Oblivion — With Carter

THE CLIFFS OF Axe Point rose like a wall beside us out from the gently swelling sea. They merged their blackness, at no great height above our heads, into the fog of swirling flakes. And the thick falling snow blurred all but the near expanse of ruffled water from our sight—blurred it (among those steep-to mountains) into murk.

There was a log jammed endways into a crevice of the rock, and we had moored the sloop to it. Then we had lit a fire in an empty oil-can, and warmed up some beans and sow-belly, and boiled some tea, and eaten a grateful meal. But our chief longing had been to warm our aching feet, that had ached with the cold since we had left the bay at Kendall's place, early that morning, before dawn. We had warmed them blissfully.

We had just cast off from the log. We were pushing on the sweeps, intending to creep forward under the shelter of Axe Point (since the wind blew from ahead) before putting out upon our next tack across the Inlet, when round the corner of the cliff there shot into sight men standing, rowing, in a small boat. The Dohertys at last! The two Doherty boys and Mike M'Curdy!

Their boat was soon alongside ours. M'Curdy fumbled under a tarpaulin and pulled a whisky bottle out. "Drink hearty, Kendall," he giggled cheerfully; "it's your own whisky. We just had to open a few bottles to keep ourselves from freezing in this blank-blank rowboat."

"You blank-blank blanks," said Kendall, but he did not mind . . .

The Dohertys had come, and therefore Kendall had no further need to journey down the Inlet in the sloop. So we took the other men aboard, and tied their boat astern, and ran before the breeze straight back to Kendall's camp. Many drinks we had upon the way. The sloop once anchored and the freight all safe ashore inside the tent, it came to someone that a howl could easily be heard at Carter's camp. So the jest was to raise a drunken hullaballoo, to torture Carter with the knowledge that there was whisky near him that he could not drink; to "rub it in" to him that Kendall, hateful Mike Kendall, was undergoing all the joys of drunkenness. You may bet that Carter and François heard and understood the noise, and that two tragic figures lay wakeful in their bunks that night.

Supper and whisky and the return to warmth after the cold endurance of the day filled us all with glee. Kendall became full of hints of a mystery; the hints soon became so broad that we divined the truth. We had a poet in our midst!!

The poet needed but a touch to burst him into song. But whether Carter (as the poet hoped) could hear the song was very doubtful. The tent door, anyway, was opened, and Kendall sang his loudest through it, and some of us thought that Carter might come lurking in the underbrush to hear. So, for the best effect, the song was sung again at intervals throughout the evening, until the singer had either become too drunk to sing or we too drunk to hear.

### CARTER: A SATIRE
by Mike Kendall
*(To the tune of "The White Cockade")*

I

As I was agoing for to *bale* my sloop,
I passed the camp and I *saw* the group,
So I came back and com*posed* this rhyme,
For they was busy splicing line.

*Chorus*

Grainger was a-firing, and the *donkey* throwing fog,
Cully at the throttle, and he *had* a big log;
Bill blew the whistle when the line it broke,
For Joe was slingin' riggin', and Carter tending hook.

## II

So they all went to supper when *it* got dark;
Them oolicans was done, but they *had* that shark,
And Carter sez, "Boys, we're *out* of luck,
For that there cook puts up poor truck."
*(Chorus.)*

## III

His steamboat was anchored right *out* in the bay;
A storm came up and she *sank* in the spray,
But Carter sez, "Don't YOU worry at all,
For I *paid* seventeen for her just last fall."
*(Chorus.)*

## IV

Pretty soon they had got all the logs off the claim,
And they went down the Inlet as poor as they came,
But Carter sez, "Boys, you'll now see a sight;
I'll put on the mitts and the bears I'll fight."
*(Chorus.)*

Perhaps the song means little to you.

That evening we four men of an audience applauded wildly; slapping Kendall on the back, trying to get him to remember more verses. For the song was full of the most deadly innuendo. It would be impossible to give you a just idea of the subtlety of the allusions, but I may try to explain one or two points.

"A group busy splicing line": Carter would ruffle at this, for such emphasis on the fact that the line had broken was a covert sneer at the man whose business it was to haul out logs without breaking the line — the hook tender. And Carter, in the song, was tending hook.

"The donkey throwing fog" calls up to any logger the picture of an old rattle-trap of a donkey-engine from every decayed point of which clouds of steam are squirting.

"Them oolicans was done." Oolicans are, like smelts, very good eating, in my opinion. But the fact that Carter had laid in a large stock of them, barrelled in brine, bought for a small sum from the Indians, gave the singer a chance to insinuate that Carter's cookhouse was run upon the cheap. A boss logger is very touchy about the reputation of his cookhouse.

As for the mud shark, it had trapped itself under some boom logs when the tide ran out. We had taken its liver to make oil.

Throwing the blame of poor meals upon the cook is an old wheeze of the mean boss. You will perceive, therefore, in the second verse, another dig at Carter.

In the last verse there is a slur that would hurt Carter. It is in the assumption that he had not been logger enough to make money up the Inlet.

The sting of the whole song, however, is in the last two lines, that are calculated, with deadly accuracy, to hurt Carter in his tenderest vanity. At a certain early stage of drink Carter will often tell a yarn about a fight he once had with a bear when out hunting on the mountains in Cariboo. It is a good, interesting yarn, and it shows signs of embellishment from time to time, for Carter enjoys telling it hugely. But in a hostile world it affords material for bitter jibes behind Carter's back — and is held an unblushing lie.

It was on the afternoon of the next day that I saw Carter for the last time. Mike Kendall and Bob Doherty had gone out hunting in the snow, and when we heard their signal shots from the mountainside beyond Carter's camp we launched a boat to fetch them and their meat home by water.

So it happened that first the three of us, and soon after (upon the return journey) the five of us, glided slowly in our rowboat past the whole line of Carter's camp and rafts and place of working. The afternoon was calm and still.

Upon a great raft, left high upon the beach, stood the old donkey-engine squirting its many puffs of steam. Just within the fringe of the seashore woods we saw a figure toiling in the snow. It was François. And, now running to and fro between François and the engine; now bending over the machinery to tighten nuts with hasty spanner; now jerking over levers to start the throbbing pistons, hauling upon a log that would not move — was a black figure of activity. Carter.

He saw us, of course; saw Kendall and me and the Dohertys and the well-known humorist M'Curdy. He saw the two deer that Kendall had so carefully exposed to view. (Not to share deer meat with a neighbour is a marked discourtesy.) He saw our silent passing by "upon the other side." But Carter, so close to us that we could see the very grease marks on his clothes, seemed rapt in work, unconscious that we existed. And François (who knew us all) did not dare to cast a look at us from where he worked nigh to the beach.

And that ends my story.

Farewell, then, to wrenching and tearing and intensity of effort; to great fatigues and physical discomforts; to sweaty work with simple tools; to trails in far-away mountain places; to rest and warmth beside log-fires in the woods!

Farewell to loggers and my youth!

Farewell to it all: marriage is better.

And now I must go and scrub the kitchen floor of
The cottage next to Mrs. Potts,
in (what will be) Lyall Avenue,
(outside the city limits of)
VICTORIA,
B.C.

*July* 1908

# Afterword

WHEN I FINISHED reading Martin Allerdale Grainger's tale of the tall timber I carried it to an honor shelf in my workroom and fitted it between Stewart Holbrook's rambunctious contribution to lumberjack folklore, *Holy Old Mackinaw,* and N. C. McDonald's salty logging novel, *Song of the Axe.*

Before long I took it off the shelf to read again the wonderful opening description of window shopping along Cordova Street in Vancouver at the turn of the century. That led to the essay (so different from Holbrook's) about the simple pleasure to be found working in the woods for wages, and then I reviewed the perilous journey of the crank *Sonora* "dingy as a London slum" in the tidal waters of Knight Inlet, which leads eastward from Queen Charlotte Strait, and the even more chancy 70-mile trip in a punky rowboat in dead winter, and before I knew it I had read the whole book again.

The central character, of course, is the anti-hero Carter, whose "desperate drive-her-under pigheadedness" so fascinated the narrator, Mart. But what of Mart, the stand-in for the author in this autobiographical novel? Grainger tells us a great deal about hand-logging in British Columbia—the working of small tracts by independent operators—but precious little about himself. We learn only that he was English, had a good education, and was physically fit, though no Rambo. But why was this educated Englishman working for wages in the dark forests of northern British Columbia? How old was he? What experiences had given him his unusual perspective?

I couldn't find Grainger in the reference books available locally. Thomas Quigley, a librarian at the Vancouver Public Library, supplied the answers.

Martin Allerdale Grainger was born in London in 1874. He went to Australia as a child when his father was appointed agent general for South Australia. He attended Cambridge on a scholarship, excelling in math; immediately after graduation, he rushed off to the Klondike. Gold eluded him, on the Yukon and in northern British Columbia. He volunteered for service in the Boer War in Africa in 1898, then returned to British Columbia where for several years he unprofitably practiced hand-logging and journalism.

While knocking about in the Gulf Islands he met and fell in love with Mabel Higgs. She went back to England. He pursued her, first by mail, then in person, finally persuading her to marry him. They wanted to return to British Columbia but he was out of money. So, using material from the letters his wife had saved, he wrote *Woodsmen of the West,* which he dedicated to his creditors. With a $300 advance from the publisher, he bought a first-class steamship ticket for Mabel, steerage passage for himself, and set off for Victoria.

Back in British Columbia, Grainger caught on as secretary of a royal commission assigned to study logging practices in the province. He wrote most of a report that led to the passage of the Forest Act of 1912 and the establishment of the B.C. Forest Service. In 1917 he was appointed Chief Forester, a position he held until 1920. He seems to have been an unconventional civil servant. When introduced to King George V he wore Indian moccasins.

In 1922 he formed his own company, Timberland Investigation and Management, which he operated successfully until he dropped dead in his doctor's office on October 15, 1941. Unfortunately he never had cause to write another book.

Although almost unknown in the United States, Grainger has not been forgotten in Canada. There is a profile of him in the *Oxford Companion to Canadian Literature.* Roderick Haig-Brown critiqued *Woodsmen* in *Canadian Literature* (No. 23: Winter 1965).

Haig-Brown noted that even in the bad old days there were independent loggers unlike the dark, angry, power-loving, ruthless

Carter. Not all despoiled the land. "There were quiet, frugal, efficient small operators out in the islands and inlets, versatile and ingenious men who nursed their simple machinery, kept their rigging in shape, survived the depressions and made money in the booms."

He adds that, in telling of a time and place and people that have been very little explored, Grainger "has preserved at least some of the ways and thought that went into the small upcoast logging camps... He is splendidly accurate in describing the drains that swallowed the schemes and drew off the dreams as well as the casual courage with which ill-equipped men accepted the enormous hazards of weather and tide and country."

*Woodsmen of the West* is said to be the first novel to use Vancouver, B.C. as part of its setting. Most of the places Grainger mentions have disappeared, but the Columbia Hotel at 303 Columbia Street is still in business. And the book is finally in print in the United States, praise be.

Murray Morgan
Auburn, Washington
July 1988

| | DATE DUE | | |
|---|---|---|---|
| | | | |
| | | | |
| | | | |
| | | | |
| | | | |
| | | | |
| | | | |
| | | | |
| | | | |
| | | | |
| | | | |